THE Rosetta Stone™

LANGUAGE LIBRARY

English I
Workbook

FAIRFIELD LANGUAGE TECHNOLOGIES

TRS-ENG1WKBK-3.0

ISBN 1-883972-46-9

Printed in the United States of America.

Imprimido en los Estados Unidos de América.

Fairfield Language Technologies
165 South Main Street
Harrisonburg, VA 22801 USA

Telephone: (540) 432-6166 (or 800-788-0822 USA and Canada)
Fax: (540) 432-0953
E-mail: info@trstone.com
Web site: www.trstone.com

Worksheet 1-01

I. Match the words with the pictures.

_____ 1. a girl

_____ 2. a man

_____ 3. a ball

_____ 4. a dog

_____ 5. a car

_____ 6. a cat

_____ 7. an airplane

_____ 8. a boy

_____ 9. a horse

_____10. a woman

A
B
C
D
E
F
G
H
I
J

II. Match the words.

_____11. man   a. airplane

_____12. car   b. girl

_____13. cat   c. woman

_____14. boy   d. dog

III. Fill in the blank.

15. _____ in a car   man

16. a boy and a girl _____ a boat   a woman

17. a boy in an _____   in

18. a girl _____   under

19. a _____ on a horse   on a horse

20. a boy _____ a ball   airplane

ENGLISH   **Introductory Nouns and Prepositions**

Worksheet 1-02

I. Match the words with the pictures.

_____ 1. The woman is swimming.

_____ 2. The horse is jumping.

_____ 3. The woman is running.

_____ 4. The girl is running.

_____ 5. The girl is jumping.

_____ 6. The man and the woman are walking.

_____ 7. The woman is reading.

_____ 8. The man is running after the boy.

_____ 9. The airplane is flying.

_____ 10. The fish is swimming.

A B C D E F G H I J

II. Possible (P) or Impossible (I)?

_____ 11. The man and the woman are dancing.

_____ 12. The fish is walking.

_____ 13. The dog is flying.

_____ 14. The bird is swimming.

_____ 15. The ball is jumping.

III. Fill in the blank.

16. The airplane is _____.

17. The _____ is swimming.

18. The _____ are reading.

19. The girls are running _____.

20. The horse is _____.

man

flying

jumping

girls

after the boy

I. Match the words with the pictures.

_____ 1. The old woman has white hair.

_____ 2. The fish is white.

_____ 3. an old car

_____ 4. The girl has black hair.

_____ 5. The man has long hair.

_____ 6. The cat is black.

_____ 7. The woman has short hair.

_____ 8. The man has very short hair.

_____ 9. a new car

_____10. The woman has long hair.

A B C D E F G H I J

II. Possible (P) or Impossible (I)?

_____11. The cat is pink.

_____12. The dog is black.

_____13. The airplane is yellow.

_____14. The house is red.

_____15. The horse is blue.

III. Fill in the blank.

16. The girl has _____ hair.   car

17. The old man has _____ hair.   black

18. The _____ is red.   white

19. The yellow airplane is _____.   man

20. The _____ has short hair.   new

ENGLISH   **Descriptive Adjectives**

I. Match the words with the pictures.

_____ 1. four and four

_____ 2. five

_____ 3. ten

_____ 4. one, two, three

_____ 5. nine

_____ 6. four, five, six

_____ 7. two

_____ 8. three, three, three

_____ 9. six, seven, eight

_____10. three

A  B

C  D  E

F  G

H  I  J

II. Write the numbers in English.

11. 10 _____

12. 2 _____

13. 4 _____

14. 9 _____

15. 6 _____

16. 8 _____

17. 5 _____

18. 0 _____

19. 1 _____

20. 7 _____

Worksheet 1-05

I. Match the words with the pictures.

_____ 1. A girl is running.

_____ 2. an eye

_____ 3. The horses are walking.

_____ 4. a baby

_____ 5. A bird is flying.

_____ 6. The car is white.

_____ 7. girls

_____ 8. Women are singing.

_____ 9. eggs

_____10. bicycles

A B

C D E

F G

H I J

II. Circle the correct word.

11. The horse   *is / are*   walking.

12. Birds   *is / are*   flying.

13. The car   *is / are*   white.

14. Women   *is / are*   singing.

15. The children   *is / are*   sitting.

III. Fill in the blank.

16. The child _____.   are blue

17. Women _____.   is flying

18. The cars _____.   is blue

19. The flower _____.   is sitting

20. A bird _____.   are singing

ENGLISH   **Singular and Plural: Nouns and Present Indicative Verbs**

I. Match the words with the pictures.

_____ 1. Two men are riding horses.

_____ 2. One man is riding a motorcycle.

_____ 3. Two girls are jumping.

_____ 4. The number is two.

_____ 5. The time is four o'clock.

_____ 6. five windows

_____ 7. There are two plates.

_____ 8. ten fingers

_____ 9. thirty fingers

_____10. The time is seven o'clock.

II. Circle the bigger number.

11. *eight / ten*

12. *nine / seven*

13. *fifteen / thirty*

14. *twenty / two*

15. *three / thirty*

III. Fill in the blank.

16. There are two _____.   four o'clock

17. The time is _____.   blue

18. One girl is _____.   plates

19. Two men _____ riding horses.   jumping

20. One plate is _____.   are

I. Match the words with the pictures.

_____ 1. Are the women sitting?

_____ 2. Is the woman running?

_____ 3. Is the airplane white?

_____ 4. Is the woman sitting?

_____ 5. Are the women running?

_____ 6. Is there a man on this house?

_____ 7. Is the fish white?

_____ 8. Is the car white?

_____ 9. Is he eating?

_____10. Is the car old?

II. Match the words.

11. Is the boy jumping? Yes, _____.   it is not

12. Is the car white? Yes, _____.   she is not

13. Is the woman sitting? No, _____.   it is

14. Is the woman running? Yes, _____.   he is

15. Is the red car old? No, _____.   she is

III. Fill in the blank with the correct question.

16. _____? Yes, it's red.

17. _____? No, the car is not black. The car is pink.

18. _____? Yes, she is.

19. _____? No, there is not.

20. _____? No, the car isn't old.

I. Match the words with the pictures.

_____ 1. bananas in a basket

_____ 2. meat

_____ 3. The man is eating.

_____ 4. The man is drinking milk.

_____ 5. apples in boxes

_____ 6. a plate with food

_____ 7. a table with no food

_____ 8. The girl is drinking milk.

_____ 9. bread

_____10. cheese

A
B
C
D
E
F
G
H
I
J

II. Match the words.

_____11. pears   a. red

_____12. strawberries   b. yellow

_____13. cheese   c. green

_____14. bananas

_____15. tomatoes

III. Fill in the blank.

16. The girl is drinking _____.   are not food

17. The boy is eating _____.   milk

18. Balls _____.   is food

19. Strawberries _____.   bread

20. Bread _____.   are food

Food, Eating and Drinking; Direct Objects   **ENGLISH**

Worksheet 1-09

I. Match the words with the pictures.

_____ 1. a black hat

_____ 2. The man and the woman are wearing bathing suits.

_____ 3. The men are wearing blue jeans.

_____ 4. The girl is not wearing socks.

_____ 5. The woman is wearing a white shirt and blue jeans.

_____ 6. The woman is wearing glasses.

_____ 7. The boy is wearing white pants.

_____ 8. The girls are wearing dresses and hats.

_____ 9. The boy is not wearing shoes.

_____10. some white hats

A B C D E F G H I J

II. Possible (P) or Impossible (I)?

_____11. The girl is wearing pants.

_____12. The horse is wearing a white skirt.

_____13. The girls are wearing raincoats.

_____14. The boy is wearing three shoes.

_____15. The woman is not wearing jeans.

III. Fill in the blank.

16. The girl _____.

17. Both women are _____.

18. The woman is _____.

19. The men _____.

20. The boy is wearing _____.

are wearing blue jeans

wearing a coat

wearing blue shirts

one hat

is wearing one shoe

ENGLISH
Clothing and Dress; Affirmative and Negative Verb Forms; Direct Objects

Worksheet 1-10

I. Match the words with the pictures.

_____ 1. Who is reading?

_____ 2. Which horse is running?

_____ 3. Who is under the table?

_____ 4. Who is drinking milk?

_____ 5. What is flying?

_____ 6. Which horse is jumping?

_____ 7. Who is eating?

_____ 8. What are the women wearing?
They are wearing white shirts.

_____ 9. Where are the bananas?

_____ 10. What food is this?
This is bread.

A
B
C
D
E
F
G
H
I
J

II. Fill in the blank.

11. Who has long hair? _____ long hair.　　these

12. What food is this? _____ are strawberries.　　the boy

13. Where is the man? The man is _____.　　the man has

14. Which child is eating bread? _____ is eating bread.　　the airplane

15. What is flying? _____ is flying.　　on the old house

III. Fill in the blank.

16. _____ horse is running? This horse is running.　　where

17. _____ is the boy doing? He is swimming.　　they

18. _____ is reading? The girl is reading.　　which

19. _____ is the white car? Here is the white car.　　who

20. What are the women wearing? _____ are wearing shirts.　　what

---

Who, What, Where, Which; Interrogative Pronouns and Adjectives　　　　**ENGLISH**

Word Search 1: 1-5

AIRPLANE
BABY
BICYCLE
BIRD
BLACK
EGG
EIGHT
ELEPHANT
EYE
FISH
FLOWER
FLYING
GIRL

HAIR
HOUSE
READING
RUNNING
SITTING
UNDER
WALKING
WHITE
WOMAN
YELLOW
YOUNG
ZERO

```
J D R B L A C K F E Y E M
I C U E B I C Y C L E Z H
A U N D E R S O R Y R E H
W N N Q L P F L O W E R A
A V I Y E L L O W B A O I
L S N O V A Y E O A D V R
K I G U B N I V W H I T E
I T Y N A E N F S A N R W
N T T G E I G H T W G B O
G I E L E P H A N T N E M
O N G I R L G H O U S E A
P G G W F B I R D T Q J N
B A B Y D B X F I S H Q I
```

Word Search 1: 6-10

BOTH
BREAD
COAT
COLOR
DARK
DRINKING
EATING
FOOD
GLASSES
HERE
MEAT
MOTORCYCLE
NUMBER

PANTS
SHIRT
SHOES
STRAWBERRIES
THERE
THESE
THEY
WATER
WHAT
WHERE
WHICH
WHO

```
C D A R K K H E R E B R F
T C I W I W H O A D R U H
S T R A W B E R R I E S F
G T M T H E R E M N A W O
L H O E E G M B T U D H O
A E T R R O P I H M T A D
S Y O E E A A P E B O T H
S Z R Y W X N Q S E E M Q
E S C O A T T W E R A W N
S H Y A X M S H I R T P P
G O C O L O R N W H I C H
D E L N M E A T Y K N E I
D S E D R I N K I N G S A
```

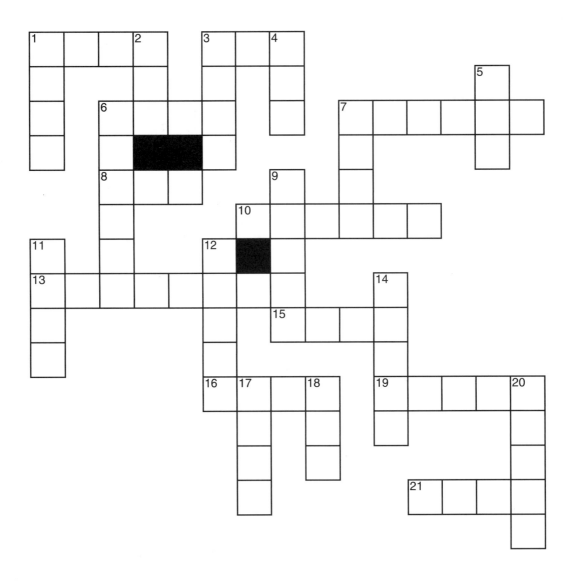

Across

1

3

6 (4)

7

8 (1)

10

13

15 (9)

16

19 (8)

21 (5)

Down

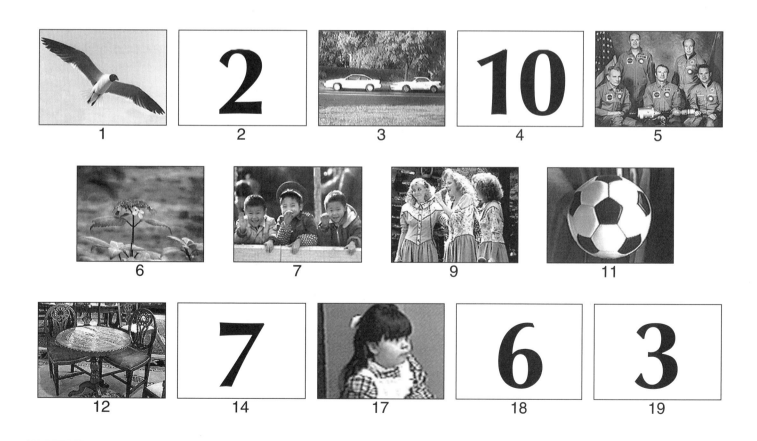

1

2 (2)

3

4 (10)

5

6

7

9

11

12

14 (7)

17

18 (6)

19 (3)

ENGLISH

Crossword 1: 6-10

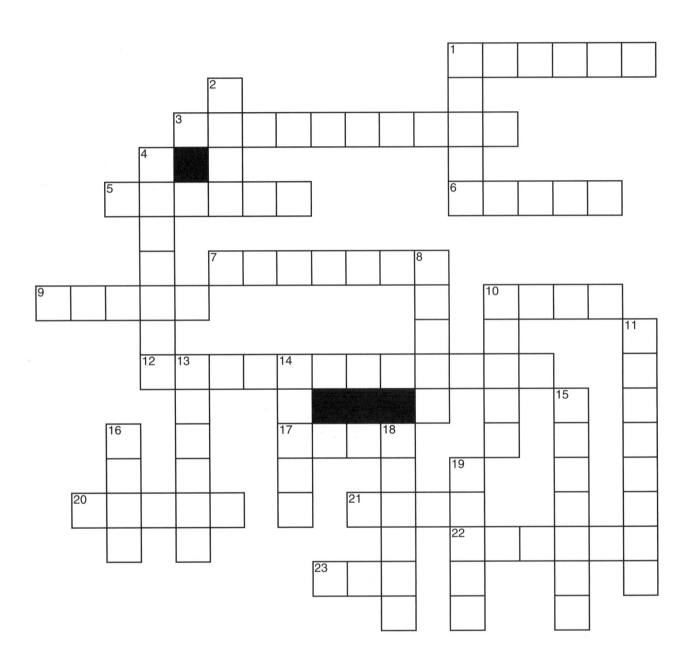

Across

1   3   5   6   7

9   10   12   17

20   21   22   23

Down

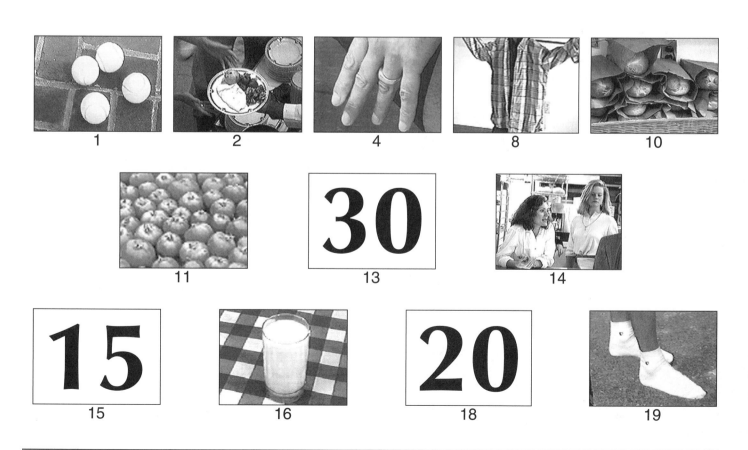

1   2   4   8   10

11   13   14

15   16   18   19

Notes

Worksheet 2-01

I. Match the words with the pictures.

_____ 1. The woman is sitting.

_____ 2. The boy is drinking.

_____ 3. The man is riding.

_____ 4. The girl is writing.

_____ 5. The birds are swimming.

A B

C D E

II. Match the words.

_____ 6. throwing

_____ 7. reading

_____ 8. eating

_____ 9. smiling

_____ 10. walking

a. laughing

b. catching

c. writing

d. running

e. drinking

III. Fill in the blank.

11. The woman is _____ on the telephone.

12. The boy is _____ the ball.

13. The birds _____.

14. The woman _____.

15. The bird _____.

are swimming

is flying

is smiling

talking

catching

IV. Describe each picture with a complete English sentence.

16. 17. 18. 19. 20.

16. _____

17. _____

18. _____

19. _____

20. _____

I. Match the words with the pictures.

_____ 1. one adult and one child

_____ 2. one person and one animal

_____ 3. two children

_____ 4. three people

_____ 5. The man is an adult.

II. Match the words.

_____ 6. animal   a. child

_____ 7. adults   b. person

_____ 8. adult   c. people

_____ 9. animals   d. children

III. Fill in the blank.

10. An elephant _____ an animal.   a man

11. A woman _____.   is

12. A fish _____ a person.   a girl

13. _____ is an adult.   is not a child

14. She is _____.   is not an adult

15. A boy _____.   is not

IV. Describe each picture with a complete English sentence.

16.   17.   18.   19.   20.

16. _____

17. _____

18. _____

19. _____

20. _____

Worksheet 2-03

I. Match the words with the pictures.

_____ 1. a big animal

_____ 2. a small car

_____ 3. a small person

_____ 4. a big wheel and a small wheel

_____ 5. a man with a big hat

A
B
C
D
E

II. Match the words.

_____ 6. big

_____ 7. old

_____ 8. white

_____ 9. short

_____10. one

a. black

b. two

c. long

d. small

e. young

III. Fill in the blank.

11. a big wheel and a _____

12. a small number _____

13. a big _____ wheel

14. a man with _____

15. a small _____

a big fish

two

umbrella

small wheel

blue

IV. Describe each picture with a complete English sentence.

16.
17.
18.
19.
20.

16. _____

17. _____

18. _____

19. _____

20. _____

Worksheet 2-04

I. Match the words with the pictures.

_____ 1. a woman with short hair

_____ 2. a woman with long hair

_____ 3. a small circle

_____ 4. The circle is bigger than the square.

_____ 5. a small square

II. Match the words.

_____ 6. longer

_____ 7. bigger

_____ 8. biggest

_____ 9. longest

_____10. big

a. smallest

b. small

c. smaller

d. shortest

e. shorter

III. Fill in the blank.

11. The red circle _____ the red square.　　is yellow

12. The biggest _____ is blue.　　biggest

13. The smallest square _____.　　is bigger than

14. The _____ circle is red.　　long

15. a woman with _____ hair　　circle

IV. Describe each picture with a complete English sentence.

16.
blue red yellow — 17.
yellow — 18.
yellow green — 19.
yellow green — 20.

16. _____

17. _____

18. _____

19. _____

20. _____

Shapes and Colors; Descriptive Adjectives: Comparative Nouns, Pronouns　　**ENGLISH**

I. Match the words with the pictures.

_____ 1. She is pointing with her right hand.

_____ 2. The window is round.

_____ 3. The girl is holding a hat in her left hand.

_____ 4. The cup is in the woman's right hand.

_____ 5. This clock is square.

A

B

C

D

E

II. Match the words.

_____ 6. left

_____ 7. round

_____ 8. his

_____ 9. both

_____10. long

a. her

b. right

c. short

d. square

e. neither

III. Fill in the blank.

11. She is _____ with her right hand.

12. The girl is _____ a hat in her left hand.

13. Two yellow balls are in her _____ hand.

14. No U-_____.

15. This sign is _____.

holding

pointing

rectangular

right

turn

IV. Describe each picture with a complete English sentence.

16.

17.

18.

19.

20.

16. _____

17. _____

18. _____

19. _____

20. _____

I. Match the words with the pictures.

_____ 1. This airplane is flying.

_____ 2. This man does not have hair.

_____ 3. The girl is drinking.

_____ 4. The boys are not jumping.

_____ 5. This man is wearing a hard hat.

A B

C D E

II. Fill in the blank.

6. The woman is wearing _____.

7. The man is riding _____.

8. The airplane is _____.

9. The woman is using the _____.

10. The boys _____.

11. This man _____.

not flying

are not jumping

a black hat

has hair

the bike

phone

III. Fill in the blank.

12. The boy is not wearing a black hat. _____.

13. The boy is not sitting in the airplane. _____.

14. The woman is not wearing a white hat. _____.

15. This girl is not walking. _____.

He is swimming.

She is wearing a black hat.

He is wearing a white hat.

She is riding the horse.

IV. Describe each picture with a complete English sentence.

16.

17.

18.

19.

20.

16. _____

17. _____

18. _____

19. _____

20. _____

Verbs: Negative Forms

ENGLISH

I. Match the words with the pictures.

_____ 1. The boy and the girl are sitting on the ground.

_____ 2. The man and the boy have balls on their heads.

_____ 3. The boy is lying on the ground.

_____ 4. The women are standing on the wall.

_____ 5. The man and the children are walking.

A

B

C

D

E

II. Match the words.

_____ 6. the man and the woman

_____ 7. the dog and the cat

_____ 8. the tomatoes and the bananas

_____ 9. red and blue

_____ 10. the shirt and the pants

a. the bread and the cheese

b. the boy and the girl

c. the shoes and the socks

d. the fish and the bird

e. green and white

III. Fill in the blank.

11. The woman and the dog are _____.

12. The women are standing in front of _____.

13. The man and the woman _____.

14. The car and the airplane _____.

15. The man and the boy are in the _____.

airplane

are red

the wall

are dancing

walking

IV. Describe each picture with a complete English sentence.

16. 17. 18. 19. 20.

16. _____

17. _____

18. _____

19. _____

20. _____

I. Match the words with the pictures.

_____ 1. This man is in front of a car.

_____ 2. The bananas are in the basket.

_____ 3. two people without glasses

_____ 4. The hat is on the boy.

_____ 5. a boy with a stick

A
B
C
D
E

II. Possible (P) or Impossible (I)?

_____ 6. The airplane is above the ground.

_____ 7. The truck is in the man.

_____ 8. The bicycle is behind the car.

_____ 9. The fish are around the diver.

_____10. The car is on the plate.

III. Fill in the blank.

11. The _____ are in the basket.

12. The people _____ the boat.

13. This boy _____ the tree.

14. The bicycle is _____.

15. The boy is on _____.

beside the car

bananas

the bicycle

are in

is behind

IV. Describe each picture with a complete English sentence.

16.
17.
18.
19.
20.

16. _____

17. _____

18. _____

19. _____

20. _____

Worksheet 2-09

I. Match the words with the pictures.

_____ 1. The man's hands are on his knees.

_____ 2. He is touching his nose.

_____ 3. a face

_____ 4. four hands

_____ 5. He is touching his mouth.

A

B

C

D

E

II. Match the words.

_____ 6. one hand's fingers

_____ 7. two hands' fingers

_____ 8. two people's fingers

_____ 9. eyes

_____ 10. two people's arms

a. 2

b. 4

c. 5

d. 10

e. 20

III. Fill in the blank.

11. This young man has food in _____.

12. He is touching his _____.

13. The man's hands _____.

14. The woman is combing _____.

15. The woman's arms are _____.

nose

his mouth

on her knees

are on his knees

the girl's hair

IV. Describe each picture with a complete English sentence.

16.

17.

18.

19.

20.

16. _____

17. _____

18. _____

19. _____

20. _____

Head, Face, Hands and Feet; Possessive Nouns and Pronouns

I. Match the words with the pictures.

_____ 1. The boy and the girls are jumping.

_____ 2. The girl has cut the paper.

_____ 3. The man is drinking the milk.

_____ 4. The horse has jumped.

_____ 5. The man is going to drink the milk.

A

B

C   D   E

II. Match the words.

_____ 6. is eating

_____ 7. is falling

_____ 8. are eating

_____ 9. are drinking

_____ 10. is drinking

a. have eaten

b. has fallen

c. has drunk

d. has eaten

e. have drunk

III. Fill in the blank.

11. The boy is going to jump _____.

12. The horse is _____.

13. The girls _____.

14. The woman _____.

15. The girl is going to _____.

into the water

are not jumping

has jumped

jumping

cut the paper

IV. Describe each picture with a complete English sentence.

16.   17.   18.   19.   20.

16. _____

17. _____

18. _____

19. _____

20. _____

Present Progressive, Present Perfect and Future with "Going To"   **ENGLISH**

Word Search 2: 1-5

ADULT
ANIMAL
BIGGEST
CIRCLE
DOWN
LAUGHING
LEFT
LITTLE
NEITHER
OTHER
PERSON
RECTANGLE
RIGHT
ROUND
SIGN
SMALL
SMALLEST
SOMETHING
SQUARE
TALKING
TELEPHONE
THAN
THAT
TRUCK
TURN

```
T H A N E I T H E R B D C
Q D L T T U R N R S I G N
S O M E T H I N G X G E L
M W J L P E R S O N G T A
A N R E C T A N G L E T U
L T I P Z K D W A I S R G
L H G H R O U N D T T U H
E A H O P X L H W T V C I
S T T N K O T D U L I K N
T X P E C I R C L E B V G
I S Q U A R E F S M A L L
A N I M A L W O T H E R A
L E F T A L K I N G B O Y
```

Word Search 2: 6-10

ABOVE
AROUND
BEHIND
BESIDE
BETWEEN
BIKE
CANDY
COMBING
DOES
DRINK
EACH
EAT
FENCE
FRONT
GOING
HAVE
HEAD
HIS
HUMAN
INTO
KNEES
MOUTH
THEIR
USING
WITHOUT

```
W F V G H F E N C E B T E
I N T O A R O K O A E A T
T H E I R O X H A C S E G
H A R O U N D B E H I N D
O V K M V T R U X C D Q O
U E C O M B I N G I E P E
T J A A G E N M O U T H S
K U N D A T K O I D S A U
C M D V A W H R N H A U S
N O Y K N E E S G N A R I
I A B O V E A Y U S I K N
N H U M A N D A H P W Q G
B U T H I S U H B I K E A
```

Crossword 2: 1-5

Across

1. not this
5. No U-____
6. laughing and _____
7. She is _____ the ball.
9. not long
12. longer than a square
13. a green fruit
16. not a square
17. It is round; there are four on a car.
19. not big
20. eight, nine, ____
21. a color

Down

1. bigger than a car
2. writing with a ___
3. not smallest
4. He is playing the _____.
8. plate and ___
9. a No Parking ____
10. adults and children
11. four o'_____
13. cup and _____
14. not left
15. not right
16. bulls and ____
18. not short

Crossword 2: 6-10

Across

2. The microphone is in the singer's left _____.
5. The girl has ___ the paper.
6. not a brush
7. not a comb
8. The dog is _____ two people.
11. A _____ is on a leg above the foot.
13. eyes, nose and mouth are on a _____
15. _____, one, two, three
16. not in front
20. The airplane is above the _____.
21. She is wearing _____ on her feet.

Down

1. People _____ food.
3. not under
4. not behind, but in _____
5. under the mouth, on a face
8. Two bowls are _____ each other.
9. The boy is behind the _____.
10. The man is touching the horse's ___.
12. His ___ is on the table.
13. kicking balls with their _____
14. Some chairs are _____ a table.
16. The cat drinks milk from a _____ .
17. The man's hands are on ___ knees.
18. The ___ is running after the car.
19. between mouth and eyes on a face

Notes

Worksheet 3-01

I. Match the words.

_____ 1. tall   a. fat

_____ 2. straight   b. younger

_____ 3. thin   c. right

_____ 4. left   d. short

_____ 5. older   e. curly

II. Describe each picture with a complete English sentence.

6.   7.   8.   9.   10.

6. _____

7. _____

8. _____

9. _____

10. _____

III. Fill in the blank.

11. Who has short, _____, black hair?   bald

12. Who has _____, straight, black hair?   curly

13. This young man has _____.   tall man

14. Who is _____?   long

15. Which _____ is wearing glasses?   short hair

IV. Yes or No?

_____16. Fat people are thin.

_____17. Bald people have curly hair.

_____18. Babies are taller than men.

_____19. Boys are shorter than men.

_____20. Women are taller than girls.

I. Match the words.

_____ 1. many   a. fat

_____ 2. thin   b. smallest

_____ 3. in front of   c. few

_____ 4. round   d. behind

_____ 5. biggest   e. rectangular

II. Describe each picture with a complete English sentence.

6.   7.   8.   9.   10.

6. _____

7. _____

8. _____

9. _____

10. _____

III. Fill in the blank.

11. There are the same number of girls _____.   than people

12. How many coins _____?   more

13. There are fewer horses _____.   as boys

14. There are _____ people than umbrellas.   tables

15. There are more chairs than _____.   are there

IV. Possible (P) or Impossible (I)?

_____16. There are many balls on the ground.

_____17. There are fewer apples than bananas in a basket.

_____18. The cowboy is riding many horses.

_____19. There are more adults than children in a car.

_____20. The man has more hands than fingers.

Worksheet 3-03

I. Match the words.

_____ 1. socks   a. eyes

_____ 2. shirt   b. feet

_____ 3. glasses   c. legs

_____ 4. pants   d. head

_____ 5. hat   e. arms

II. Describe each picture with a complete English sentence.

6.   7.   8.   9.   10.

6. _____

7. _____

8. _____

9. _____

10. _____

III. Fill in the blank.

11. The man _____ is wearing a sweater.   dress

12. She is wearing a red _____ sweater.   blue pants

13. The woman is wearing a red _____.   and white

14. He is _____ pants.   with glasses

15. The boy is wearing _____.   putting on

IV. Possible (P) or Impossible (I)?

_____16. The man's shorts are longer than his pants.

_____17. The woman is putting on a dress.

_____18. The dog is wearing pants.

_____19. The woman is wearing a yellow top.

_____20. The baby is not wearing anything.

Worksheet 3-04

I. Match the words.

_____ 1. jumping   a. on the telephone

_____ 2. throwing   b. a ball

_____ 3. talking   c. a skirt

_____ 4. wearing   d. an apple

_____ 5. eating   e. rope

II. Describe each picture with a complete English sentence.

6.   7.   8.   9.   10.

6. _____

7. _____

8. _____

9. _____

10. _____

III. Fill in the blank.

11. This is the _____ of a house.   the table

12. The children are _____ the table.   are outside

13. The boy is sitting at _____.   outside

14. Which children _____?   are

15. The children _____ playing jump rope. standing on

IV. Possible (P) or Impossible (I)?

_____16. The fish is running.

_____17. The bird is flying.

_____18. The cow is jumping rope.

_____19. The building is sitting.

_____20. The boy is sitting at the table.

I. Match the words.

_____ 1. grass   a. white

_____ 2. banana   b. red

_____ 3. strawberries   c. yellow

_____ 4. milk   d. orange

_____ 5. carrot   e. green

II. Describe each picture with a complete English sentence.

| 6. | 7. | 8. | 9. | 10. |

6. _____

7. _____

8. _____

9. _____

10. _____

III. Fill in the blank.

11. a _____ and white cat   red

12. _____ grass   horse

13. pink _____   brown

14. a yellow, a _____ and a pink flower   flowers

15. Which is the black _____?   green

IV. Yes or No?

_____16. People have two arms.

_____17. Ten is more than five.

_____18. Zero is more than six.

_____19. People have ten fingers.

_____20. Cats have two legs.

I. Match the words.

_____ 1. two legs

_____ 2. no legs

_____ 3. four legs

_____ 4. many legs

_____ 5. eight legs

a. two dogs

b. a person

c. a herd of goats

d. a lion

e. a fish

II. Describe each picture with a complete English sentence.

6.	7.	8.	9.	10.

6. _____

7. _____

8. _____

9. _____

10. _____

III. Fill in the blank.

11. The camel is standing on _____ legs.

12. The white tiger is _____.

13. A bird is _____.

14. This horse _____ real.

15. Two cows _____.

climbing

is not

four

are running

flying

IV. Yes or No?

_____16. The kangaroo is an animal.

_____17. The lion is a person.

_____18. The giraffe is a small animal.

_____19. The dragon is not a real animal.

_____20. The rocking horse is not a real horse.

Worksheet 3-07

I. Match the words.

_____ 1. cold   a. weak

_____ 2. strong   b. sad

_____ 3. hungry   c. hot

_____ 4. happy   d. healthy

_____ 5. sick   e. full

II. Describe each picture with a complete English sentence.

6. _____

7. _____

8. _____

9. _____

10. _____

III. Fill in the blank.

11. She is tired. _____ is not tired.   a. they

12. Someone is _____.   b. and the dog

13. The boy _____ are happy.   c. he

14. _____ are hot and tired.   d. is hungry

15. The woman _____.   e. hungry

IV. Possible (P) or Impossible (I)?

_____16. The rocking horse is thirsty.

_____17. The sick man is healthy.

_____18. The bird is ugly.

_____19. The hungry girl is full.

_____20. The babies are not strong.

Worksheet 3-08

I. Match the words.

_____ 1. dentist

_____ 2. teacher

_____ 3. mechanic

_____ 4. baker

_____ 5. doctor

a. car

b. bread

c. sick person

d. teeth

e. student

II. Describe each picture with a complete English sentence.

6.

7.

8.

9.

10.

6. _____

7. _____

8. _____

9. _____

10. _____

III. Fill in the blank.

11. The mechanic is fixing the _____.

12. The dentist is working on _____.

13. The man is proud _____.

14. This man is getting money _____.

15. The doctor is _____ of the man.

of his son

in a bank

the man's teeth

taking care

car

IV. Possible (P) or Impossible (I)?

_____16. The baby is fixing a car.

_____17. The nurse is taking care of a woman.

_____18. The mechanic is fixing a truck.

_____19. The secretary is typing.

_____20. Someone is baking an umbrella.

Professions and Conditions: Descriptive Adjectives   **ENGLISH**

Worksheet 3-09

I. Match the words.

_____ 1. a real man a. a statue of a rabbit

_____ 2. real flowers b. a statue of a horse

_____ 3. a group of people c. a picture of people

_____ 4. a real horse d. a picture of a man

_____ 5. a real rabbit e. a picture of flowers

II. Describe each picture with a complete English sentence.

6.   7.   8.   9.   10.

6. _____

7. _____

8. _____

9. _____

10. _____

III. Fill in the blank.

11. The hat is on his _____.   hands

12. These are _____ flowers.   head

13. Her _____ are covering her eyes.   the wall

14. The pictures are on _____.   is a statue

15. Which man on a horse _____?   real

IV. Yes or No?

_____16. Some pictures are on walls.

_____17. The picture is jumping rope.

_____18. People have three arms.

_____19. Elephants have four legs.

_____20. The hand has five fingers.

Worksheet 3-10

I. Match the words.

_____ 1. four fifteen   a. 3:30

_____ 2. two o'clock   b. 7:45

_____ 3. a quarter past seven   c. 4:15

_____ 4. three thirty   d. 2:00

_____ 5. a quarter to eight   e. 7:15

II. Describe each picture with a complete English sentence.

6.   7.   8.   9.   10.

6. _____

7. _____

8. _____

9. _____

10. _____

III. Fill in the blank.

11. It is six _____.   quarter

12. It is a _____ to eight.   past

13. It is just past _____.   almost

14. It is a quarter _____ seven.   o'clock

15. It is _____ five o'clock.   five o'clock

IV. Yes or No?

_____16. Eleven o'clock is after ten o'clock.

_____17. A quarter past seven is after eight o'clock.

_____18. Six thirty is after six o'clock.

_____19. Eight o'clock is after nine thirty.

_____20. A quarter to seven is after seven o'clock.

Word Search 3: 1-5

ANOTHER
ANYTHING
BALD
BLOND
BUILDING
COINS
CURLY
FEWER
GRASS
GROUP
HOW
INSIDE
LOAF

LOAVES
MANY
MORE
OUTSIDE
PUTTING
SAME
SEVERAL
SHORTS
STRAIGHT
SWEATER
UMBRELLAS
YOUNGER

```
M U F X C O I N S U A H S
A A E T P U T T I N G O F
N S W E A T E R A M X W Z
Y P E L J S T R A I G H T
T Y R Q E I C P L M O R E
H O L M M D A N O T H E R
I U M B R E L L A S G M P
N N Z A X O S E V E R A L
G G B L O N D L E Q O N O
R E L D S A M E S O U Y A
A R S H O R T S C F P F F
S I N S I D E Z C U R L Y
S N B U I L D I N G A D K
```

Word Search 3: 6-10

AFRAID
AFTERNOON
ALMOST
BEAUTIFUL
COLD
DOCTOR
FIXING
HAPPY
HEALTHY
HUNGRY
MONEY
MORNING
NIGHT

PAIN
POLICE
QUARTER
SICK
SOMEONE
STRONG
STUDENT
TEACHER
THIRSTY
TIRED
UGLY
WEAK

```
A S B M G R P O L I C E P
H I E Q T T I R E D O N A
U C A N E Z R D S P H W I
N K U I A N U O O M A E N
G P T G C L M C M O P A W
R C I H H S O T E R P K F
Y A F T E R N O O N Y S H
Z Q U A R T E R N I U T E
R D L F N K Y X E N G U A
R S T R O N G S S G L D L
V J A A L M O S T F Y E T
F I X I N G R U C W N N H
C O L D C W T H I R S T Y
```

Crossword 3: 1-5

Across

2. a building
6. This is the outside of the _____.
8. She is wearing blue jeans, a purple _____, and a hat.
10. not outside
11. The girl is jumping _____.
12. There are _____ horses than people.
17. not older
18. She is not wearing _____; she is wearing shorts.
20. no hair
21. not fat
22. they are dancing

Down

1. not short
2. small, round money
3. rain _____
4. not curly
5. The boys are playing _____.
7. A _____ of runners.
9. A man is _____ than a boy.
13. _____ color is the egg?
14. not straight
15. pink flowers and green _____
16. There are _____ chairs than tables.
18. There are the ___ number of girls as boys.
19. Her _____ is long.
20. The woman has _____ hair.

Crossword 3: 6-10

Across

1. not cold
3. not happy
4. _____ is in a bank.
6. She is taking _____ of the man.
7. A dentist works on _____.
8. He has fallen; he is in _____.
11. not afternoon or night
12. The camel is standing on two _____.
14. The _____ is cooking.
16. a big cat
19. Money is in a _____.
20. He is _____ of his car.

Down

1. He is wearing a ___ on his head.
2. not a student
3. There are the ___ number of boys as girls.
5. not weak
8. a pink animal
9. The _____ and doctor care for sick people.
10. The doctor cares for the _____ man.
13. The man is proud of his _____.
15. not new
16. He is running. He is hot and _____.
17. Outside there is green _____ on the ground.
18. He has money. He is _____.
19. not a man

Notes

Worksheet 4-01

I. Answer with Yes or No.

1. Is a pony bigger than a horse?_____

2. Is a girl younger than a woman? _____

3. Is a violin playing a boy? _____

4. Is a dog playing the guitar? _____

5. Is a dog a fish?_____

6. Is a fish drinking milk? _____

7. Is a statue playing with a dog?_____

8. Is a fish riding a bicycle? _____

9. Is an adult taller than a child? _____

10. Is a violin an animal? _____

11. Is a bear an animal?_____

12. Is a house a building? _____

13. Is a church a building? _____

14. Is a man sitting and running? _____

15. Is an elephant putting on a sweater? _____

II. Describe each picture with a complete English sentence.

| 16. | 17. | 18. | 19. | 20. |

16. _____

17. _____

18. _____

19. _____

20. _____

Worksheet 4-02

I. Answer the question with a complete English sentence.

Example: Are the woman's feet apart? *No, the woman's feet are not apart.*

1. Is the car door open? No,_____

2. Are the woman's eyes closed? Yes, _____

3. Are the statue's eyes closed? No, _____

4. Is the window open? No, _____

5. Is the man's hand closed? Yes, _____

6. Are the man's hands together? No, _____

7. Are the boy's legs together? Yes, _____

8. Are the fish and the car together? No, _____

9. Are the boys together? Yes, _____

10. Are the woman's arms straight? Yes, _____

11. Is the girl's hand open? No, _____

12. How many toes does a baby have? _____

13. How many legs does a lion have? _____

14. How many eyes does a person have? _____

15. How many arms does a person have?_____

II. Describe each picture with a complete English sentence.

| 16. | 17. | 18. | 19. | 20. |

16. _____

17. _____

18. _____

19. _____

20. _____

Open–Closed, Together–Apart, Straight–Bent

ENGLISH

Worksheet 4-03

I. Write each number in English.

1. 8 _____

2. 11 _____

3. 20 _____

4. 4 _____

5. 13 _____

6. 5 _____

7. 15 _____

8. 30 _____

9. 80 _____

10. 50 _____

II. Write each number in English.

11.   12.   13.   14.   15.

16.   17.   18.   19.   20.

11. _____

12. _____

13. _____

14. _____

15. _____

16. _____

17. _____

18. _____

19. _____

20. _____

I. Answer with Yes or No.

1. Can a plant talk? _____

2. Can a boy talk on a mobile phone? _____

3. Can a man who is drinking talk? _____

4. Can a woman who is underwater talk? _____

5. Can a turtle talk? _____

6. Can a mannequin talk on the phone? _____

7. Can a boy talk to his dog? _____

8. Can a dog talk to a boy? _____

9. Is a walkie-talkie a motorcycle? _____

10. Can a bird play chess?_____

11. Can a baby read a book?_____

12. Is a phone an animal? _____

13. Can some men wear yellow shirts? _____

14. Can some girls wear bathing suits? _____

15. Can older women talk to younger women? _____

II. Describe each picture with a complete English sentence.

| 16. | 17. | 18. | 19. | 20. |

16. _____

17. _____

18. _____

19. _____

20. _____

People and Talking   **ENGLISH**

Worksheet 4-05

I. Answer with Yes or No.

1. Can a horse come out of a van? _____

2. Can dogs go up a wall? _____

3. Can airplanes go up a wall? _____

4. Can babies sleep? _____

5. Can pictures sleep? _____

6. Can people go down an escalator? _____

7. Can cars go down an escalator? _____

8. Can people go up the stairs? _____

9. Can airplanes go up the stairs? _____

10. Can girls come out of the water? _____

11. Can men go up a ladder? _____

12. Can babies go up a ladder? _____

13. Can cats sleep? _____

14. Can rectangles sleep? _____

15. Can flowers sleep? _____

II. Describe each picture with a complete English sentence.

| 16. | 17. | 18. | 19. | 20. |

16. _____

17. _____

18. _____

19. _____

20. _____

I. Answer with Yes or No.

1. Can men climb steps? _____

2. Can men climb steps while putting on their shoes?_____

3. Can women point? _____

4. Can a hat smile? _____

5. Can boys smell flowers? _____

6. Can glasses watch TV? _____

7. Can girls ride horses? _____

8. Can girls ride horses while watching TV? _____

9. Can people sing while playing the piano? _____

10. Can some people play the guitar? _____

11. Can people go up an escalator? _____

12. Can some people march in a parade?_____

13. Can boxes march in a parade? _____

14. Can a baby drive a car? _____

15. Can a goat eat flowers while reading a book? _____

II. Describe each picture with a complete English sentence.

| 16. | 17. | 18. | 19. | 20. |

16. _____

17. _____

18. _____

19. _____

20. _____

I. Answer with Yes or No.

1. Are a brother and a sister in the same family? _____

2. Are a mother and a father parents? _____

3. Are a husband and wife a couple? _____

4. Is a mother's son her child? _____

5. Is a father's daughter his son? _____

6. Are two girls a brother and sister? _____

7. Can parents have more than one child? _____

8. Is a father a girl? _____

9. Is a father bigger than a baby? _____

10. Is a father older than his daughter? _____

11. Is a boy younger than his mother? _____

12. Can a father talk to his child? _____

13. Can a girl talk to her mother? _____

14. Are there four people in some families? _____

15. Is a mother a boy? _____

II. Describe each picture with a complete English sentence.

| 16. | 17. | 18. | 19. | 20. |

16. _____

17. _____

18. _____

19. _____

20. _____

Worksheet 4-08

I. Answer with Yes or No.

1. Can anybody sleep?_____

2. Can everybody ride a horse? _____

3. Can anybody talk on the phone? _____

4. Can a fish talk on the phone? _____

5. Can anybody take a picture? _____

6. Can someone take a picture? _____

7. Can everybody jump rope? _____

8. Can anybody jump rope? _____

9. Can somebody ride a horse? _____

10. Can everything walk? _____

11. Can somebody run? _____

12. Can everybody swim underwater? _____

13. Can a horse run while nobody is riding it? _____

14. Can cats sleep while nobody is watching? _____

15. Can children eat while nobody is watching? _____

II. Describe each picture with a complete English sentence.

| 16. | 17. | 18. | 19. | 20. |

16. _____

17. _____

18. _____

19. _____

20. _____

Everybody, Somebody, Someone, Nobody, Anybody   **ENGLISH**

Worksheet 4-09

I. Answer with Yes or No.

1. Is an antique car old? _____

2. Is a submarine a car? _____

3. Can everybody drive a limousine? _____

4. Are submarines in buildings? _____

5. Are trains going up steps? _____

6. Are some cars parked? _____

7. Are cars in accidents? _____

8. Are trains parked in front of a house? _____

9. Are boats in the water? _____

10. Can anybody put a bike on a van? _____

11. Can anybody get into a van? _____

12. Are cars in the water? _____

13. Are boats on mountains? _____

14. Are cars on bridges? _____

15. Are elephants getting into a trolley? _____

II. Describe each picture with a complete English sentence.

| 16. | 17. | 18. | 19. | 20. |

16. _____

17. _____

18. _____

19. _____

20. _____

ENGLISH   **Vehicles; Related Verbs and Prepositions**

Worksheet 4-10

I. Answer with Yes or No.

1. Can some singers use a microphone?_____

2. Can children play with their friends? _____

3. Can some children play without their friends? _____

4. Can flowers play jump rope? _____

5. Can some people carry elephants? _____

6. Can people with umbrellas walk?_____

7. Can apples run? _____

8. Can some people eat shirts? _____

9. Can people wear hats inside? _____

10. Can dogs play in the grass?_____

11. Can anybody play in the sand? _____

12. Can anybody sit on a box? _____

13. Can anybody wear a bathing suit? _____

14. Can someone talk on the telephone? _____

15. Can somebody wear a hat inside? _____

II. Describe each picture with a complete English sentence.

| 16. | 17. | 18. | 19. | 20. |

16. _____

17. _____

18. _____

19. _____

20. _____

Prepositions and Objects of Prepositions: With and Without　　　　　　**ENGLISH**

Word Search 4: 1-5

ABOUT
ALL
APART
ASLEEP
AWAKE
BECAUSE
BOOK
CLOSED
COME
COUPLE
DOOR
EIGHTEEN
ENTERING

FATHER
FOURTEEN
LEAVING
NOW
OPEN
PLANT
SLEEPING
SMILE
STAIRS
STEPS
TOGETHER

```
A L E A V I N G V F V L U
S H A B E C A U S E D N P
T J P S L E E P I N G A S
A W A K E C F A U T A S I
I O R D I O A P F E H L D
R I T O G E T H E R W E E
S C T O H L H S M I L E D
F O U R T E E N Y N X P A
O U I I E O R H S G R A B
O P E N E B S C T N O W O
A L L W N C O M E U S J U
G E B B O O K D P L A N T
S B I R U C L O S E D G I
```

Word Search 4: 6-10

ACCIDENT
ANY
BRIDGE
BROTHER
DAUGHTER
ELECTRIC
EVERYBODY
FAMILY
FRIENDS
HUSBAND
LISTENING
MOTHER
MOUNTAIN

NOBODY
NONE
NOTHING
ONTO
PARENTS
PURSE
RIVER
SAND
THROUGH
WATCHING
WHILE
WIFE

```
O N G W R B R I D G E G E
N O T H I N G L U S L B V
O N R I V R M O T H E R E
N E E L E J O F X E C O R
W I F E R P U R S E T T Y
T L I S T E N I N G R H B
A D A U G H T E R E I E O
F A M I L Y A N Y O C R D
C Q T A C C I D E N T K Y
N O B O D Y N S Y T O S B
P A R E N T S F X O Q A B
T H R O U G H U S B A N D
W A T C H I N G P F Y D M
```

Crossword 4: 1-5

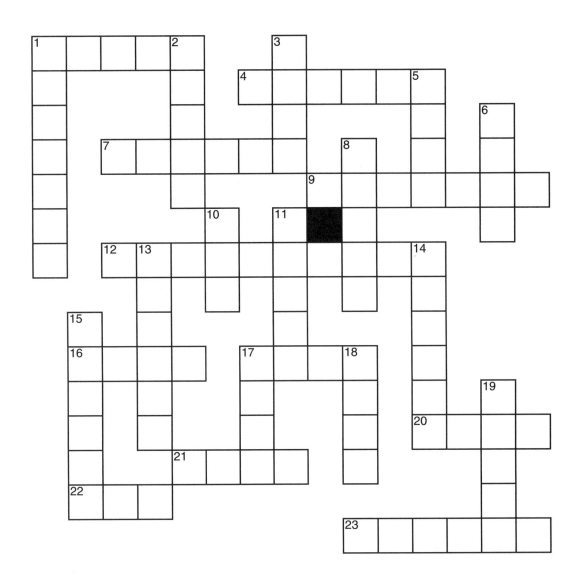

Across

1. People are going up the ____.
4. two people
7. mother and _____
9. The couple is _____.
12. The girl is swimming _____.
16. not closed
17. The woman's arms are ____.
20. These women can't _____.
    They are mannequins
21. He is riding a _____.
22. The boy is cooking an ____.
23. sixty, seventy, ____

Down

1. fourteen, fifteen, _____
2. forty, fifty, ____
3. The car ___ is open.
5. Her ___ are open.
6. a small horse
8. thirty, forty, _____
10. eight, nine, _____
11. not asleep
13. seventy, eighty, _____
14. a small animal with long ears
15. The man is talking on the ____ phone.
17. The girl is reading a ____.
18. There are five ___ on each foot.
19. A flower is a kind of _____.

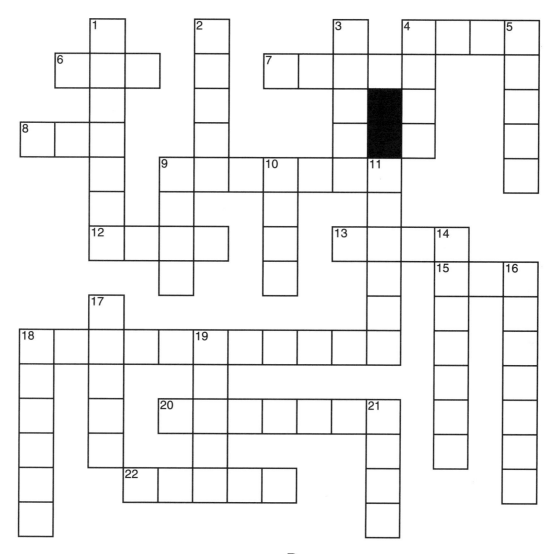

Across

4. husband and _____
6. bigger than a car, smaller than a truck
7. There is no food on the ___.
8. not no
9. There is ___ on the plate.
12. These men are carrying ___ while they are walking through the water.
13. a piece of furniture to sit on
15. This man can't talk ___.
18. They are wearing helmets while riding their _____.
20. mother and father
22. twenty, thirty, _____

Down

1. The car is ___ a truck on the road; it is going to be in front of the truck.
2. She is playing the _____.
3. longer than a truck; has many cars
4. not strong
5. not full
9. ___ of the boys are jumping.
10. a horse's foot
11. He is cold and is wearing _____.
14. The car is very old; it is an _____ car
16. This car has been in an accident. It is _____.
17. She is going down the _____.
18. a woman who has a child
19. smaller than a sofa
21. ____ is white and cold.

Notes

I. Fill in the blank.

1. One plus three equals _____.   two
2. Eight minus two equals _____.   one
3. Ten divided by five equals _____.   six
4. Two times six equals _____.   five
5. Six minus five is _____.   eight
6. Three plus four is _____.   four
7. Four times _____ equals twenty.   three
8. Two times _____ equals sixteen.   eleven
9. Fifteen divided by _____ equals five.   twelve
10. Six plus _____ is seventeen.   seven

II. Match the word with its symbol.

____11. minus   a. =
____12. equals   b. +
____13. times   c. −
____14. plus   d. / or ÷
____15. divided by   e. x

III. Write in English.

16. 20 _____

17. 4 + 5 = 9 _____

18. 15 / 5 = 3 _____

19. 12 − 7 = 5 _____

20. 2 x 8 = 16 _____

I. Fill in the blank.

1. The woman is walking her _____.   girl's

2. The _____ shirt is white.   too

3. _____ is walking three dogs.   dog

4. This shirt _____ the boy's shirt. It is too big.   black

5. The woman's horse is not jumping. It _____ standing.   someone

6. The woman's hat is _____.   is small

7. The man is wearing _____ shirt.   his own

8. It is _____ small.   table

9. The man's dog _____.   is

10. The man's box is on the _____.   is not

II. Write a complete English sentence using one or more words from the list.

dark haired	too	children's	women's
blond haired	child's	adults'	clothing
own	adult's	men's	bucking

11. _____

12. _____

13. _____

14. _____

15. _____

III. Describe each picture with a complete English sentence.

16.	17.	18.	19.	20.

16. _____

17. _____

18. _____

19. _____

20. _____

I. Fill in the blank.

1. The man is going to _____ the mobile phone.   airplane

2. The dog is _____ catch the frisbee.   thrown

3. The _____ is flying.   flapping

4. The children are going to _____ off the table.   opened

5. The woman has _____ the ball.   use

6. The woman has _____ to sleep.   climbing

7. The bird is _____ its wings.   going to

8. The camel has _____ its mouth.   hat

9. The dog has picked up the _____.   jump

10. The man in the white shirt is _____ the wall.   gone

II. Write a complete English sentence using one or more words from the list.

ride	thrown	hug	work	wings	frisbee
drawer	gone	hugging	flapping	catch	pick
opened	sleep	done	its	caught	picked

11. _____

12. _____

13. _____

14. _____

15. _____

III. Describe each picture with a complete English sentence.

16.	17.	18.	19.	20.

16. _____

17. _____

18. _____

19. _____

20. _____

ENGLISH   **Present Progressive, Present Perfect and Future with "Going To"**

Worksheet 5-04

I. Write the numbers in English.

1.   16   _____

2.   38   _____

3.   43   _____

4.   154   _____

5.   352   _____

6.   425   _____

7.   696   _____

8.   281   _____

9.   926   _____

10. 1078   _____

11. 2857   _____

12. 1875   _____

13. 3123   _____

14. 7154   _____

15. 9239   _____

16.   59   _____

17.   549   _____

18.   734   _____

19. 1087   _____

20. 10125   _____

I. Fill in the blank.

1. The woman is giving the boy _____.   from

2. The woman is giving money _____.   with her dog

3. The man is giving _____ medicine.   of water

4. The woman is getting medicine _____ the man.   taking

5. The woman is playing _____.   to the boy

6. The woman is climbing _____.   hat

7. The man is drinking the glass _____.   money

8. The girl is wearing a _____.   the woman

9. The girl is _____ a plate.   gave

10. The man _____ a glass of milk to the woman.   the stairs

II. Write a complete English sentence using one or more words from the list.

| pushing | mat | giving | from |
| cart | glass | medicine | gave |

11. _____

12. _____

13. _____

14. _____

15. _____

III. Describe each picture with a complete English sentence.

16.   17.   18.   19.   20.

16. _____

17. _____

18. _____

19. _____

20. _____

I. Fill in the blank.

1. The sun is _____ on the woman.   it is hot

2. Snow _____ the mountains.   the summer

3. The match _____ a yellow fire.   sun

4. People play in the water when _____.   is covering

5. People play in the snow when _____.   ice

6. The sun is _____ the clouds.   shining

7. The _____ is hot.   smoke

8. _____ is cold.   behind

9. The fire is making black _____.   it is cold

10. It is hot in _____.   makes

II. Write a complete English sentence using one or more words from the list.

fire	candle	burning	making	match	scarves	day
sun	trees	clouds	makes	summer	play	shining
ice	mountains	smoke	stove	winter	when	

11. _____

12. _____

13. _____

14. _____

15. _____

III. Describe each picture with a complete English sentence.

16.   17.   18.   19.   20.

16. _____

17. _____

18. _____

19. _____

20. _____

Worksheet 5-07

I. Fill in the blank.

1. Trees are a kind of _____.   apples
2. Bread is a kind of _____.   animal
3. Sheep are a kind of _____.   a flower
4. Horses and cats are _____.   ducks
5. _____ are animals.   plant
6. _____ are a kind of fruit.   cheese
7. _____ is a kind of plant.   food
8. _____ is a kind of food.   is a kind of plant
9. Bushes and flowers _____.   animals
10. Grass _____.   are kinds of plants

II. Write a complete English sentence using one or more words from the list.

kind	duck	ice cream
kinds	ducks	cattle
plants	bushes	

11. _____

12. _____

13. _____

14. _____

15. _____

III. Describe each picture with a complete English sentence.

16.   17.   18.   19.   20.

16. _____

17. _____

18. _____

19. _____

20. _____

Worksheet 5-08

I. Fill in the blank.

1. A chair is a piece of _____.   musical instruments

2. A jacket is a piece of _____.   dress

3. Guitars are _____.   electric piano

4. A _____ is a piece of furniture to sit on.   clothing

5. A _____ is a piece of clothing.   tables

6. _____ are musical instruments.   furniture

7. A _____ is a piece of furniture to sleep on.   getting dressed

8. Someone is playing an _____.   bed

9. The clown is _____.   sofa

10. _____ are furniture.   flutes

II. Write a complete English sentence using one or more words from the list.

furniture	bed	bench	holds	dressed	musical	violins	bass
piece	desk	clothes	jacket	formal	instruments	flute	drums
pieces	sit	dresser	tie	music	saxophone	flutes	drummer

11. _____

12. _____

13. _____

14. _____

15. _____

III. Describe each picture with a complete English sentence.

16.   17.   18.   19.   20.

16. _____

17. _____

18. _____

19. _____

20. _____

Furniture, Clothing and Instruments   **ENGLISH**

Worksheet 5-09

I. Fill in the blank.

1. There are _____ tables than chairs.   only

2. There is _____ of food on this tray.   too many

3. There are _____ birds to count.   count

4. There are _____ a few flowers.   two people

5. We can _____ the boys: one, two, three.   a lot

6. There is _____ water than land in this picture.   there are

7. _____ are on one bicycle.   fewer

8. There are only a _____ of animals.   the same

9. _____ too many hats to count.   less

10. There is _____ amount of milk in the glasses.   couple

II. Write a complete English sentence using one or more words from the list.

amount	lot	count	candles
less	land	we	only
tray	boys		

11. _____

12. _____

13. _____

14. _____

15. _____

III. Describe each picture with a complete English sentence.

16. 17. 18. 19. 20.

16. _____

17. _____

18. _____

19. _____

20. _____

Worksheet 5-10

I. Fill in the blank.

1. This man is scratching _____.   is crying

2. The boy _____ because he is sad.   tongue

3. The woman is _____. She is at a funeral.   nose

4. This man is _____ his shoe.   off the ground

5. This boy is sticking out his _____.   his neck

6. The boy's arms _____.   is tired

7. The man is blowing his _____.   sad

8. The boy is yawning because he _____.   are folded

9. The child is picking up something _____.   in a race

10. This man is going to run _____.   tying

II. Write a complete English sentence using one or more words from the list.

waving	sticking	tying	thinking	picking	win	neck	string
coughing	yawning	scratching	stretching	funeral	won	forehead	tongue
sneezing	blowing	crying	finishing	race	medals	kite	folded

11. _____

12. _____

13. _____

14. _____

15. _____

III. Describe each picture with a complete English sentence.

16.   17.   18.   19.   20.

16. _____

17. _____

18. _____

19. _____

20. _____

I. Fill in the blank.

1. We are _____ and tired.	hair
2. I am a _____ with a red head.	we
3. I am wearing _____.	is tired
4. I have red _____.	are happy
5. I _____ healthy.	tired
6. We are running and _____ are tired.	am
7. We are running and we are _____.	a hat
8. I am the man _____.	bird
9. We are not tired. He _____.	who is hungry
10. We _____.	hot

II. Write a complete English sentence using one or more words from the list.

I	hungry	unhappy	thirsty	healthy
you	full	who	we	weak
am	tired	cold	not	sick

11. _____

12. _____

13. _____

14. _____

15. _____

III. Describe each picture with a complete English sentence.

16.	17.	18.	19.	20.

16. _____

17. _____

18. _____

19. _____

20. _____

Word Search 5: 1-5

BACK
CATCH
CAUGHT
CLOTHING
DIVIDED
DONE
DRAWER
EQUALS
FROM
GAVE
GIVING
GLASS
GONE

MEDICINE
MINUS
OWN
PLUS
POCKET
RIDE
SLEEP
TIMES
USE
WALKED
WINGS
WORK

```
P L U S L M S J F O W B L
V C S H W Y G L Y B A C K
Q M E D I C I N E A L Z U
Y I D O N E V L V J K F X
U N T W G D I V I D E D P
Q U F N S E N C C N D R I
I S L E E P G L A S S A N
G A V E L R K O U J F W P
C Q P O C K E T G O R E H
K E Q U A L S H H W O R K
G T X L T D M I T I M E S
H X H V C G O N E H Y Q S
Y B J Q H P J G R I D E Z
```

Word Search 5: 6-11

AMOUNT
COUGHING
COUNT
DRESSED
FINISHING
FOREHEAD
FUNERAL
FURNITURE
ICE
INSTRUMENTS
JACKET
LAND
MUSIC

ONLY
PIECE
SCRATCHING
SUMMER
THINKING
TIE
TONGUE
UNHAPPY
WHEN
WINTER
YAWNING
YOU

```
N W D M U S I C P I E C E
O F R G S C S U M M E R F
F U E D C O U N T X Y A O
I N S T R U M E N T S D R
N E S W A G T N Y O U I E
I R E I T H I N K I N G H
S A D N C I E J M C H F E
H L D T H N K H T E A A A
I U S E I G W H E N P E D
N F U R N I T U R E P L T
G T O N G U E O N L Y A D
J A C K E T G A M O U N T
W O Y A W N I N G O B D D
```

Crossword 5: 1-5

Across

2. Three _____ five is eight.
6. not thin
7. Two ___ six equals twelve.
9. The doctor gave him _____.
11. The man ___ a glass of milk to the woman.
12. He will ___ the food.
14. not a man
16. a ___ haired woman
21. It has _____ its mouth.
22. He will ___ the phone.
23. Nine plus seven _____ sixteen.
24. The bird is flapping its _____

Down

1. He will ___ the ladder.
3. there are ___ fingers on a hand
4. The dog is going to _____ the frisbee.
5. six times two
7. ___ are climbing.
8. They are sitting on a ____.
10. Eight _____ by two is four.
13. one, two, ___
15. Six ____ two is four.
17. He will ___ the bicycle.
18. one, two, three, ____
19. The man is drinking a ____ of milk.
20. four plus three

Crossword 5: 6-11

Across

1. The tie is around his _____.
4. They go in the water _____ it is hot.
6. There are ___ a few flowers.
9. coat
12. Guitars are musical _____.
14. ___ is cold.
15. not hot
17. a piece of furniture to sleep on
20. The fire is making black _____.
21. They ran in a _____.
22. The boy is holding the kite _____ in his mouth.

Down

1. She was running, but ___ she isn't.
2. Grass is a _____ of plant.
3. a long, thin musical instrument
5. A dresser is a piece of furniture that ___ clothes.
7. table, bed, and chair
8. A match _____ fire.
10. a _____ of furniture
11. The ___ is hot.
13. The ___ is around his neck.
16. a kind of bird
17. a piece of furniture to sit on
18. not night
19. Someone is playing the ___.
20. He will ___ on the sofa.

I. Fill in the blank.

1. This man is in a bike _____.   hat

2. The boy is on _____.   mouth is

3. The man has a _____ on his head.   people

4. He is _____ the wall.   race

5. The boy's _____ open.   clown

6. The cup is _____.   a frisbee

7. The _____ has a hat on his head.   the table

8. The boy is in _____.   full

9. The _____ were in a parade.   the airplane

10. The dog has _____ in its mouth.   climbing

II. Describe each picture with a complete English sentence.

11.   12.   13.   14.   15.

11. _____

12. _____

13. _____

14. _____

15. _____

III. Match the words.

____16. is holding   a. was in the water

____17. had a hat   b. were in a parade

____18. are in a parade   c. was holding

____19. was inside   d. has a hat

____20. is in the water   e. is inside

ENGLISH   **To Be and To Have: Present and Past Tenses**

Worksheet 6-02

I. Fill in the blank.

1. The boy is going to _____ the ball.　　　looking

2. The woman _____ the man.　　　put

3. The boy is _____ at the ball.　　　the steps

4. The boy _____ into the water.　　　enter

5. The woman has _____ something into the bag.　　　is kissing

6. The woman is going to _____ the store.　　　trunk

7. The man has closed the _____ of the car.　　　has slid

8. The people are going up _____.　　　throw

9. The boy has _____.　　　the carriage

10. The man is getting into _____.　　　fallen

II. Describe each picture with a complete English sentence.

11.　　　　12.　　　　13.　　　　14.　　　　15.

11. _____

12. _____

13. _____

14. _____

15. _____

III. Match the words.

_____16. throw　　　　a. the street

_____17. cross　　　　b. a person

_____18. come down　　　　c. the steps

_____19. kiss　　　　d. the trunk of a car

_____20. close　　　　e. a ball

Present Progressive, Present Perfect and Future with "Going To"　　　**ENGLISH**

I. Fill in the blank.

1. The woman with _____ has an earring.   is bald

2. The girl has black hair and dark _____.   long hair

3. This person has a beard, but no _____.   statue

4. The old man has a _____ beard.   skin

5. These people are wearing _____.   dressed

6. The man _____.   does not

7. These men are _____ up.   white

8. The woman _____ have a beard.   bald

9. The _____ man has a beard.   moustache

10. The _____ has a moustache.   uniforms

II. Describe each picture with a complete English sentence.

11.   12.   13.   14.   15.

11. _____

12. _____

13. _____

14. _____

15. _____

III. Match the words.

_____16. short   a. dark

_____17. light   b. long

_____18. is bald   c. has hair

_____19. a beard   d. a person

_____20. a statue   e. a moustache

I. Fill in the blank.

1. an empty paper _____   bouquet

2. many _____ of apples   empty

3. a _____ of paper towels   bag

4. _____ of watermelon   bottle

5. a _____ of flowers   gloves

6. a _____ of boots   roll

7. a full _____ of juice   potato chips

8. a pair of _____ and a pair of shoes   slices

9. a bag of _____   boxes

10. an _____ glass bottle   pair

II. Describe each picture with a complete English sentence.

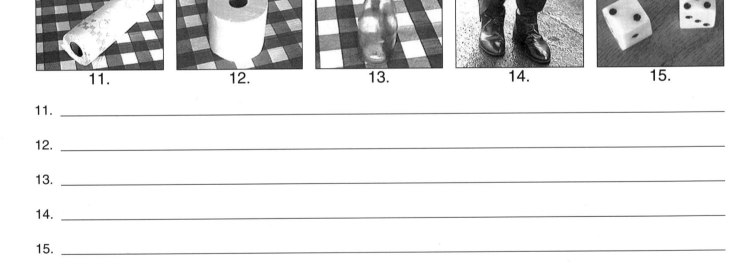

| 11. | 12. | 13. | 14. | 15. |

11. _____

12. _____

13. _____

14. _____

15. _____

III. Match the words.

_____16. loaves   a. toilet paper

_____17. roll   b. flowers

_____18. bottle   c. boots

_____19. bouquet   d. juice

_____20. pair   e. bread

Worksheet 6-05

I. Fill in the blank.

1. The bus is up on the _____.   anymore

2. The woman is singing and _____ the piano.   drums

3. The woman _____ the horse.   sidewalk

4. The woman is _____ on the phone.   both

5. _____ the man and boy are wearing hats.   bicycles

6. These women are playing _____ and smiling.   are singing

7. The men are riding _____.   playing

8. _____ of these people is singing.   talking

9. The clown is not dressing _____.   is riding

10. All six of these people _____.   neither

II. Describe each picture with a complete English sentence.

11.
12.
13.
14.
15.

11. _____

12. _____

13. _____

14. _____

15. _____

III. Match the words.

_____16. talking   a. the piano

_____17. riding   b. on the phone

_____18. playing   c. food

_____19. eating   d. hats

_____20. wearing   e. a motorcycle

I. Fill in the blank.

1. The man is playing the _____.   traffic

2. The man is wearing a shirt that is too _____.   yawning

3. The _____ light is red.   wearing

4. The man has _____ the ladder.   frisbee

5. These people are in a bike _____.   climbed

6. The man is _____ his own shirt.   is fishing

7. The boy _____.   race

8. The dog is carrying the _____.   small

9. The dog is _____.   are digging

10. The father and his sons _____.   guitar

II. Describe each picture with a complete English sentence.

   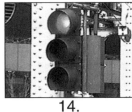 

| 11. | 12. | 13. | 14. | 15. |

11. _____

12. _____

13. _____

14. _____

15. _____

III. Match the words.

_____16. drive   a. light

_____17. traffic   b. keys

_____18. car   c. a ladder

_____19. bike   d. race

_____20. climb   e. a truck

Verbs: Present and Past Tenses; Relative Pronouns   **ENGLISH**

Worksheet 6-07

I. Fill in the blank.

1. Jake is _____ a balloon.   in a tree

2. The man on the left is _____ Charles.   the wall

3. Nancy Reagan is _____ at the singers.   holding

4. Melissa is going to _____ up the steps.   girl

5. She is a _____.   touched

6. Pranav is standing _____.   named

7. Prince Charles _____ with Ronald Reagan.   Mikhail

8. Their feet have not _____ the ground.   smiling

9. The man's name is _____.   is shaking hands

10. Melissa and Pranav are stepping onto _____. walk

II. Describe each picture with a complete English sentence.

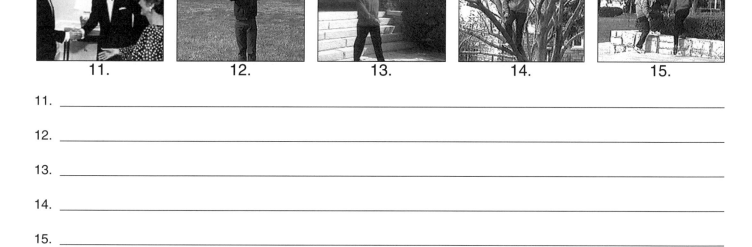

| 11. | 12. | 13. | 14. | 15. |

11. _____

12. _____

13. _____

14. _____

15. _____

III. Match the words.

____16. woman's name   a. Charles

____17. man's name   b. Melissa

____18. stepping   c. talking

____19. speaking   d. bicycle

____20. bike   e. walking

I. Fill in the blank.

1. The man _____ a shirt.   thrown

2. The girl is _____ water on her head.   kiss

3. The boy is _____ the ball.   talking

4. The woman is reading the _____.   pouring

5. The man is going to _____ his wife.   falling

6. The woman _____ the horse.   kicking

7. The boy is _____.   read

8. The woman has _____ the ball.   is putting on

9. The woman is going to _____ the book.   newspaper

10. The girl is _____ to the man.   is riding

II. Describe each picture with a complete English sentence.

| 11. | 12. | 13. | 14. | 15. |

11. _____

12. _____

13. _____

14. _____

15. _____

III. Match the words.

____16. preparing   a. a newspaper

____17. reading   b. water

____18. pouring   c. a ball

____19. climbing   d. food

____20. kicking   e. a ladder

Present Progressive, Present Perfect and Future with "Going To"   **ENGLISH**

I. Fill in the blank.

1. a _____ of bananas   escalator

2. a set of Russian _____   pair

3. a couple going down an _____   few

4. a set of _____ room furniture   single

5. a _____ grape   bouquet

6. a _____ balloons   chess

7. a _____ of flowers   dining

8. a _____ set   of gloves

9. a pair _____   dolls

10. a _____ of dice   bunch

II. Describe each picture with a complete English sentence.

| 11. | 12. | 13. | 14. | 15. |

11. _____

12. _____

13. _____

14. _____

15. _____

III. Match the words.

_____16. single   a. two

_____17. none   b. three or more

_____18. couple   c. one

_____19. lots   d. zero

_____20. a few   e. many

Worksheet 6-10

I. Fill in the blank.

1. The woman is _____ by flowers.   singer

2. The girl _____.   singing alone

3. The woman is _____ with the choir.   surrounded

4. Someone is walking alone down the _____.   crowd

5. The woman is _____ while playing the piano.   singing

6. The _____ is singing with a friend.   buildings

7. Several people are _____ against each other.   is alone

8. The church is surrounded by other _____.   puppy

9. The girl is with her _____.   racing

10. A huge _____ of people is racing.   steps

II. Describe each picture with a complete English sentence.

11.   12.   13.   14.   15.

11. _____

12. _____

13. _____

14. _____

15. _____

III. Match the words.

_____16. reading   a. books

_____17. singing   b. not surrounded

_____18. many people   c. baby dog

_____19. alone   d. crowd

_____20. puppy   e. choir

Alone, Crowd, Friend; Passive Voice of Verbs   **ENGLISH**

Worksheet 6-11

I. Fill in the blank.

1. I am _____ the bank.   typewriter

2. I am wearing a _____.   foot

3. I am _____ on someone's teeth.   cook

4. My _____ hurts.   police

5. I am hot and _____.   proud

6. I am typing on the _____.   hat

7. I am _____ the students.   working

8. I am a _____.   thirsty

9. I am _____ of my son.   teaching

10. I am at the _____ station.   outside

II. Describe each picture with a complete English sentence.

| 11. | 12. | 13. | 14. | 15. |

11. _____

12. _____

13. _____

14. _____

15. _____

III. Match the words.

_____16. ouch   a. doctor

_____17. nurse   b. bread

_____18. baking   c. car

_____19. repairing   d. students

_____20. teaching   e. hurt

Word Search 6: 1-5

ANYMORE
BEARD
BOOTS
BOTTLE
BOUQUET
CHIPS
EARRING
ENTER
HALF
LIGHT
MOUSTACHE
PAIR
PLASTIC

POTATO
PUT
ROLLS
SIDEWALK
SKIN
STORE
STREET
THEM
TOILET
TOWEL
UNIFORM
WRITE

```
C M F J R A G B O T T L E
E A R R I N G X N H B P T
P M O U S T A C H E X L D
U G E N T E R H X M S A H
T P A I R M T I J J I S X
H A L F E J T P O T A T O
B W A O E O D S Y S V I V
E F F R T O I L E T U C W
A N Y M O R E M B O O T S
R O L L S S I D E W A L K
D T J B B O U Q U E T R I
U L I G H T G R P L O D N
W M N W R I T E S T O R E
```

Word Search 6: 6-11

AGAINST
ALONE
ANYONE
AWAY
BEING
CROWD
FRIEND
HEAVY
HUGE
HURTS
KEYS
NAMED
NEWSPAPER

PAIRS
POLICEMAN
POUR
PUPPY
REPAIRING
SAYS
SINGLE
SURROUND
TOOLS
TRAFFIC
WHOLE
YEARS

```
H U R T S P A I R S B P U
E Z E R E P A I R I N G L
A H P A L O N E S N A I V
V E U F T L F M N G M G S
Y S P F R I E N D L E V U
U L P I M C H G S E D B R
W J Y C N E W S P A P E R
A Z P H Y M X L B K B N O
W H O L E A G A I N S T U
A U U R A N Y O N E L O N
Y G R C R O W D Z F Q O D
K E Y S S A Y S K T G L E
F B N O K B E I N G W S B
```

Crossword 6: 1-5

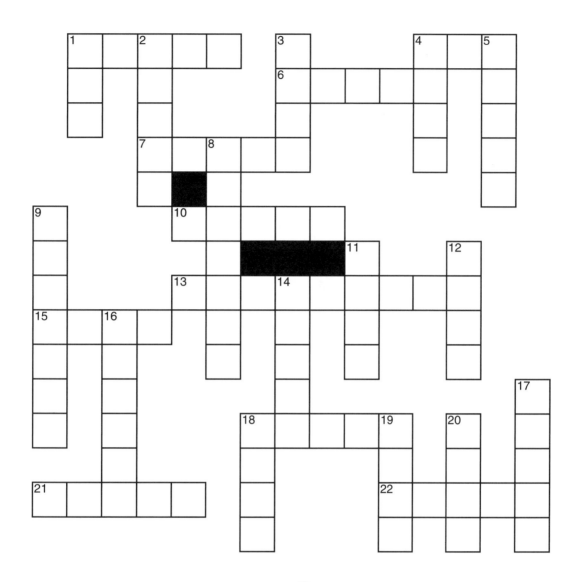

Across

1. loaves of _____
4. The boy ___ jumped.
6. a kind of fruit
7. The man is closing the ____ of the car.
10. not dark
13. He has a beard but no _____.
15. The woman is going to ____ the man.
18. hair on a man's chin
21. She is going to _____ the store.
22. potato ____

Down

1. The apples are in a ___.
2. not full
3. Children play in the _____.
4. The man has a hat on his ____.
5. The woman is entering a clothing ____.
8. He is wearing a _____.
9. She is ____ at him with her eyes.
11. He is climbing the ____.
12. not more
14. They are going to ____ into the water.
16. The people are crossing the ___.
17. People will ___ the street.
18. A person with no hair is ____.
19. a pair of ____
20. The sun makes her ____ dark.

Crossword 6: 6-11

Across

1. The _____ light is red.
4. She is going to read some _____.
9. very big
10. a _____ is using a microphone
11. There are more birds _____ tigers.
14. Flowers _____ the woman.
17. husband and _____
19. My _____ is Sandra.
20. a set of _____
22. The runners are _____ against each other.
23. She is going to _____ up the cat.

Down

2. She is not with other people. She is _____.
3. The man is closing the ___ of the car.
5. a father and several of his _____
6. "Ouch! That _____ my foot!"
7. a _____ in a race
8. She is reading the _____.
10. Jake ___, "Look at my balloon!"
12. a _____ of grapes
13. There is only one grape; it is a _____ grape
14. a ___ of tools
15. She will ___ the newspaper.
16. ___ room furniture
18. There are many singers; it is a _____ of singers
21. The girl is lying on her _____.

Notes

Notes

Worksheet 7-01

I. Fill in the blank.

1. The father is reading to his _____.   by dirt

2. The boy is flying a _____.   ground

3. The man is trying to _____.   the boat

4. The boy has been hit _____.   sons

5. The father has a shovel in one hand and a book _____.   down

6. The girl is going to give hay _____.   working

7. The girl is getting into _____.   fly a kite

8. The boy is looking _____.   kite

9. There are three kites on the _____.   in the other

10. The man is not _____.   to the horses

II. Answer the question with Yes or No.

11. Do people read newspapers? _____

12. Do birds fly kites? _____

13. Can a clown fly a kite? _____

14. Can an elephant drive a car? _____

15. Can horses work? _____

III. Describe each picture with a complete English sentence.

16.	17.	18.	19.	20.

16. _____

17. _____

18. _____

19. _____

20. _____

Worksheet 7-02

I. Fill in the blank.

1. These birds have _____.   hands

2. The swan is flapping _____.   four

3. Clocks have _____.   spread their wings

4. The workman is wearing _____.   carrying someone

5. Camels have _____ legs.   space suits

6. Bicycles have _____.   sells sunglasses

7. This horse is _____.   ships

8. Astronauts wear _____.   its wings

9. Sailors live on _____.   a hard hat

10. This person _____.   wheels

II. Answer the question with Yes or No.

11. Do clocks have hands? _____

12. Do camels have four legs? _____

13. Do dogs usually wear clothing? _____

14. Do birds have wings? _____

15. Do bicycles wear sunglasses? _____

III. Describe each picture with a complete English sentence.

| 16. | 17. | 18. | 19. | 20. |

16. _____

17. _____

18. _____

19. _____

20. _____

More Verbs; Interrogative Adjectives and Pronouns; Usually   **ENGLISH**

Worksheet 7-03

I. Fill in the blank.

1. The _____ is skiing very slowly.   walking slowly

2. _____ moving quickly across the street.   is not moving

3. This is an _____ moves fast.   skier

4. The horse is not running fast. It is _____.   someone is

5. The swimmer is in the water, but he is not _____.   swimmer

6. The biker is _____ slowly.   the woman

7. The statue _____.   boy is

8. _____ is running fast.   swimming now

9. The _____ skiing fast.   riding

10. The _____ is moving through the water.   animal that

II. Answer the question with Yes or No.

11. Can a dog run fast? _____

12. Can a skater hold still? _____

13. Can a horse put on skates? _____

14. Can a lion ski? _____

15. Can a bird fly fast? _____

III. Describe each picture with a complete English sentence.

16.   17.   18.   19.   20.

16. _____

17. _____

18. _____

19. _____

20. _____

Worksheet 7-04

I. Fill in the blank.

1. It is _____. The trees are yellow and the leaves are on the ground.   green

2. It is _____. Snow is on the trees.   sunrise

3. It is _____. The people are in the swimming pool.   fall

4. It is _____. The trees are pink and white.   moon

5. It is not cold. The trees are _____.   wintertime

6. It is cold. The trees are _____.   a road

7. The sun is coming up. We call this _____.   summertime

8. The sun is going down. We call this _____.   sunset

9. We see the _____ at night.   springtime

10. The car is on _____ between the green trees.   covered with snow

II. Answer the question with Yes or No.

11. Is there snow on the trees in the summer? _____

12. Do we see the moon at night?_____

13. Are leaves yellow in the spring? _____

14. Are the trees green in the summer? _____

15. Is it cold in the winter? _____

III. Describe each picture with a complete English sentence.

16.   17.   18.   19.   20.

16. _____

17. _____

18. _____

19. _____

20. _____

Worksheet 7-05

I. Fill in the blank.

1. _____ animals are horses.   of these ducks

2. Neither child is a _____.   most of

3. One of these _____ is a bird, but the other is not.   both

4. All of the _____ yellow.   girl

5. _____ the people are wearing yellow hats.   are white

6. All _____ have black heads.   neither

7. One _____ pointing, but the other is not.   animals

8. _____ are ducks.   flowers are

9. _____ child is a girl.   both birds

10. Some of these flowers are yellow and the others _____.   person is

II. Answer the question with Yes or No.

11. Are all flowers blue? _____

12. Are some flowers yellow? _____

13. Are most flowers black? _____

14. Are some apples green? _____

15. Is a horse an animal? _____

III. Describe each picture with a complete English sentence.

16.

17.

18.

19.

20.

16. _____

17. _____

18. _____

19. _____

20. _____

Worksheet 7-06

I. Fill in the blank.

1. All of _____ are boys.

2. One person is drinking _____.

3. This _____ is a dog.

4. _____ is not a child.

5. One of these people _____.

6. The woman is drinking milk, but the girl _____.

7. All of these animals _____.

8. _____ of these people are women.

9. Both _____ are drinking milk.

10. These two people are _____.

is not

orange juice

these children

this person

of these people

riding horses

animal

is drinking milk

are cows

II. Answer the question with Yes or No.

11. Are all animals fish? _____

12. Are all people women? _____

13. Are all boys children? _____

14. Can some people ride horses? _____

15. Are both men and women people? _____

III. Describe each picture with a complete English sentence.

16.   17.   18.   19.   20.

16. _____

17. _____

18. _____

19. _____

20. _____

None and Both; Demonstrative Adjectives   **ENGLISH**

Worksheet 7-07

I. Fill in the blank.

1. There is a circle around _____.

2. All of the people _____.

3. Most of the people _____ white.

4. The chairs are around the _____.

5. This building is not _____.

6. The boy is _____.

7. Most of the squares are _____.

8. All of the circles _____ the rectangle.

9. A square is _____.

10. A ball _____.

are wearing yellow hats

not round

are around

is round

are wearing

beside the circle

table

behind the tree

this rectangle

round

II. Answer the question with Yes or No.

11. Is a ball square? _____

12. Is a rectangle round? _____

13. Are all buildings round? _____

14. Are some clocks square? _____

15. Are some windows round? _____

III. Describe each picture with a complete English sentence.

| 16. | 17. | 18. | 19. | 20. |

16. _____

17. _____

18. _____

19. _____

20. _____

I. Fill in the blank.

1. The boy is kicking with his _____.

2. The man is _____ with his right hand.

3. There are many people on the left, but only a few on the _____.

4. The tree on the right has _____.

5. Someone is walking in front of the doors in _____.

6. The man's left hand is full _____.

7. The glass on _____ has milk in it.

8. The glass is full of _____.

9. The glass is _____.

10. The glass on the right _____.

the left

the middle

is empty

many white flowers

left foot

orange juice

right

pointing

full of milk

of candy

II. Answer the question with Yes or No.

11. Do many people write with their right hands? _____

12. Are all glasses empty? _____

13. Are all glasses full of orange juice? _____

14. Do most people kick with their hands? _____

15. Do some people point with their left hands? _____

III. Describe each picture with a complete English sentence.

| 16. | 17. | 18. | 19. | 20. |

16. _____

17. _____

18. _____

19. _____

20. _____

I. Fill in the blank.

1. The airplane is flying in front of _____.   are adults

2. _____ is riding a bicycle.   the setting sun

3. Many people are _____, but only a few are going up.   is being used

4. The airplane is flying _____.   taken

5. The bridge is above the _____.   nobody

6. Nobody is sitting _____.   only a few

7. Only one of these telephones _____.   coming down

8. Most of these people are children, but a few _____.   in a chair

9. Most of the chairs are _____. Only a few are empty.   road

10. There are _____ balloons in the sky.   above the clouds

II. Answer the question with Yes or No.

11. Are all telephones being used? _____

12. Can airplanes fly above the clouds? _____

13. Do some birds fly below the clouds? _____

14. Are some people sitting down? _____

15. Can an airplane fly behind the sun? _____

III. Describe each picture with a complete English sentence.

| 16. | 17. | 18. | 19. | 20. |

16. _____

17. _____

18. _____

19. _____

20. _____

ENGLISH   **Prepositions: Above and Below, etc.**

I. Fill in the blank.

1. The boy is _____ a mountain.   to jump over

2. The boy is _____ underwater.   climb

3. The cowboy is _____ the calf.   catch

4. She is using a _____ to take a picture.   up the tree

5. The boy is going _____ the sticks.   swimming

6. The cowboy is _____ to catch the calf.   lifting

7. He is using a rope to _____ the mountain.   pen

8. The dog is trying to _____ the frisbee.   climbing

9. He is using a _____ to write.   trying

10. The children are climbing _____.   camera

II. Answer the question with Yes or No.

11. Can you look through a window? _____

12. Can you look through a person? _____

13. Can a cow climb a tree? _____

14. Do you use a pen to take a picture? _____

15. Can a dog sing? _____

III. Describe each picture with a complete English sentence.

16.   17.   18.   19.   20.

16. _____

17. _____

18. _____

19. _____

20. _____

Worksheet 7-11

I. Fill in the blank.

1. I am _____ the bread.   together

2. We are all jumping _____.   we have

3. I am cutting _____.   the milk

4. I am going to _____.   am eating

5. _____ eaten some of the bread.   going to eat

6. I am going to drink _____.   they

7. I _____ the bread.   falling

8. I have _____.   jumped

9. I am _____.   the paper

10. I have jumped. _____ have not jumped. fall

II. Answer the question with Yes or No.

11. Do you cut milk? _____

12. Do you drink paper? _____

13. Can people eat bananas? _____

14. Can people jump over sticks? _____

15. Can bananas jump over sticks? _____

III. Describe each picture with a complete English sentence.

16.   17.   18.   19.   20.

16. _____

17. _____

18. _____

19. _____

20. _____

Word Search 7: 1-5

ACROSS
BEEN
CARRY
COVERED
DIRT
DOWNHILL
FAST
GIVE
HIT
MOON
MOST
MOVES
OTHERS

PART
QUICKLY
ROAD
SLOWLY
SOLDIERS
SOMETIMES
SPRING
STILL
SUNRISE
USUALLY
WARM
WEAR

```
J W A R M E D N S F A S T
B E E N O S U N R I S E F
G K V M S P A R T O O S U
I D I R T R V P M O V E S
S O M E T I M E S L L O U
H W Y X O N S L O W L Y A
I N M G D G P F L E I N L
T H W E A R O A D S Q G L
G I V E K D Q U I C K L Y
M L D C O V E R E D Y B N
O L P D X V A C R O S S F
O B N O T H E R S Z I V W
N C A R R Y E S T I L L T
```

Word Search 7: 6-11

ABOVE
ACROSS
BELOW
BOTH
CALF
CAMERA
CANNOT
CIRCLES
DOORS
FELL
LEANING
LIFTING
MIDDLE

OVER
RIGHT
ROUND
SETTING
SKY
SQUARES
STICKS
TAKEN
TELEPHONES
TRIANGLES
USED
WRITTEN

```
E L E A N I N G O C L X C
C M Y P C K B R R I G H T
C A N N O T E N U O V E R
M C A L F D L U Y W O I I
I R O U N D O C A M E R A
D O O R S C W R I T T E N
D S N K T I S E T T I N G
L S Q U A R E S S A D U L
E T Y N K C F H L B X S E
S I U T E L E P H O N E S
N C J E N E L T J V Z D H
S K Y K V S L Z O E U B E
V S B O T H L I F T I N G
```

Crossword 7: 1-5

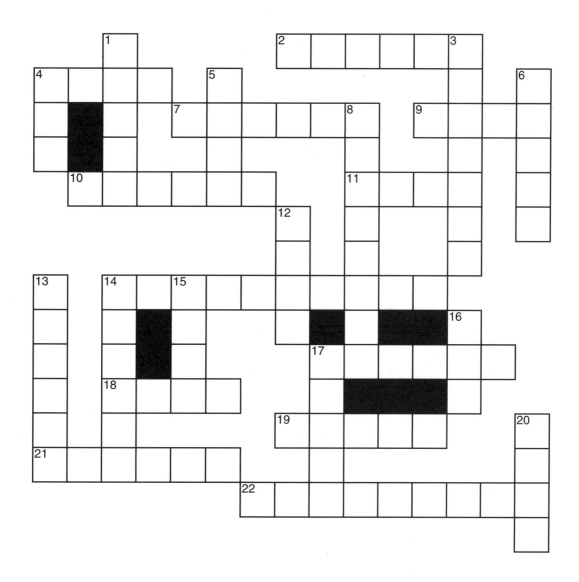

Across

2. A bicycle has two _____.
4. We ____ this a sunset.
7. The bird has its wings _____.
9. She will _____ hay to the cow.
10. She is _____ downhill.
11. It is not cold in the springtime; it is _____.
14. In the _____ it is hot.
17. not fast
18. The young men in the blue suits ____,
    but they aren't singing now.
19. They are trying to fly _____.
21. He has _____ out of the water.
22. _____ can fly.

Down

1. a color
3. a person in the water
4. an animal
5. ____ the door.
6. An astronaut _____ a space suit.
8. He is skiing _____ very fast.
12. Most of the flower is red,
    but _____ of it is yellow.
13. He is _____ to fly a kite.
14. the sun going down
15. We see the _____ at night.
16. Birds can ____.
17. The _____ is skiing downhill.
20. almost all

Crossword 7: 6-11

Across

3. not above
6. _____ live in the water.
7. The cat is going to ___ its food.
8. The horse is running ____.
9. not squares
10. Three is a ____.
12. On which ___ of the doors is the man.
15. People are talking on _____.
17. A ___ of milk.
19. It is almost night. The sun is _____.
20. The woman is using a pen to ____.
21. The time is two o'_____.
22. not circles
23. There are a few balloons in the ___.

Down

1. The strong man is ____ the big box.
2. This is not a real person; it is a ___ of a person.
4. not under
5. She is using a camera to ___ a picture.
9. The cowboy ____ ride the bull; he has fallen.
11. He is throwing the ____.
13. The car ___ are open.
14. The boy ___ off the horse.
15. She has ____ a picture.
16. He is between the dogs. He is in the ____.
18. The boy is jumping over the ____.

Notes

Notes

Worksheet 8-01

I. Describe each picture with a complete English sentence.

1.   2.   3.   4.   5.

1. _____

2. _____

3. _____

4. _____

5. _____

II. Yes or No?

____ 6. Three and four are numbers.

____ 7. Five and elephant are numbers.

____ 8. Five is the third number in 115.

____ 9. Four is the second number in 404.

____10. Six is the first number in 674.

____11. Seven is the first and last number in 707.

____12. We count: one, two, three, four, five, six.

____13. We count: five, six, eight, nine, ten.

____14. Zero is a number.

____15. A cat is not a number.

III. Write a complete English sentence using one or more words from the list.

first   third   last
second   fourth   numbers

16. _____

17. _____

18. _____

19. _____

20. _____

ENGLISH   Ordinal Numbers

I. Describe each picture with a complete English sentence.

| 1. | 2. | 3. | 4. | 5. |

1. _____

2. _____

3. _____

4. _____

5. _____

II. Yes or No?

_____ 6. Loaves of bread carry umbrellas.

_____ 7. Some people can ride horses.

_____ 8. Some people can sing.

_____ 9. Animals can play drums.

_____10. Hats can talk on the phone.

_____11. Some people can play the piano.

_____12. Nobody can sit.

_____13. All statues are smiling.

_____14. Nobody can ride a bicycle.

_____15. Everybody has a moustache.

III. Write a complete English sentence using one or more words from the list.

| riding | singing | eating | playing | carrying | kissing |
| running | dressing | talking | standing | walking | wearing |

16. _____

17. _____

18. _____

19. _____

20. _____

Worksheet 8-03

I. Describe each picture with a complete English sentence.

| 1. | 2. | 3. | 4. | 5. |

1. _____

2. _____

3. _____

4. _____

5. _____

II. Yes or No?

_____ 6. All triangles are shapes.

_____ 7. Mannequins are not real women.

_____ 8. Astronauts are mannequins.

_____ 9. A triangle is a shape.

_____10. Red, blue, and green are colors.

_____11. All birds are pink.

_____12. All shapes are circles.

_____13. All squares look like triangles.

_____14. Almost all astronauts have blue hair.

_____15. All shapes are squares.

III. Write a complete English sentence using one or more words from the list.

| like | shapes | lower |
| looks | upper | ones |

16. _____

17. _____

18. _____

19. _____

20. _____

Worksheet 8-04

I. Describe each picture with a complete English sentence.

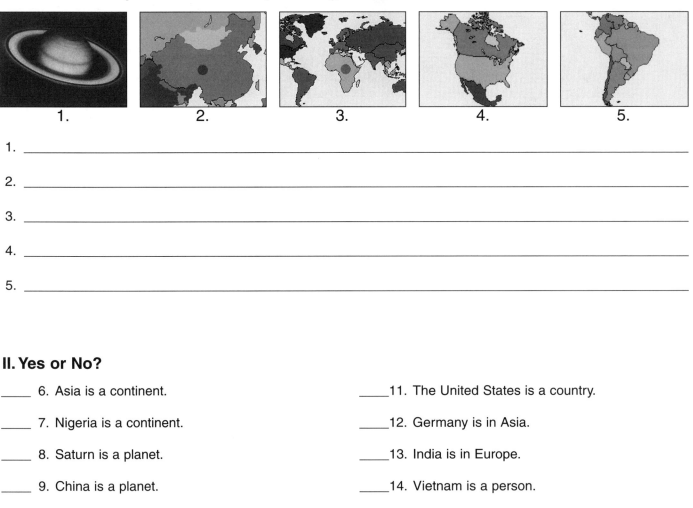

1.
2.
3.
4.
5.

1. _____

2. _____

3. _____

4. _____

5. _____

II. Yes or No?

_____ 6. Asia is a continent.

_____ 7. Nigeria is a continent.

_____ 8. Saturn is a planet.

_____ 9. China is a planet.

_____10. Africa is a country.

_____11. The United States is a country.

_____12. Germany is in Asia.

_____13. India is in Europe.

_____14. Vietnam is a person.

_____15. Egypt is on Saturn.

III. Write a complete English sentence using one or more words from the list.

called	map	Asian	Chile	Nigeria	Italy	Russia
planet	Saturn	Europe	Venezuela	Egypt	India	United Kingdom
country	Africa	European	Canada	Algeria	Vietnam	North America
continent	China	Brazil	Mexico	Tanzania	Korea	South America
colored	Asia	Argentina	Japan	Germany	Spain	United States

16. _____

17. _____

18. _____

19. _____

20. _____

I. Describe each picture with a complete English sentence.

1.
2.
3.
4.
5.

1. _____

2. _____

3. _____

4. _____

5. _____

II. Yes or No?

_____ 6. Most cars drive on the sidewalk.

_____ 7. Some bridges cross over roads.

_____ 8. People can cross railroad tracks.

_____ 9. Birds can cross sidewalks.

_____ 10. A cow can cross a street on a bicycle.

_____ 11. A wheelchair can fly.

_____ 12. People walk on the sidewalk.

_____ 13. Some cars are parked on the street.

_____ 14. All streets are empty.

_____ 15. All sidewalks are full of people.

III. Write a complete English sentence using one or more words from the list.

highway	toward	alley	hole
crosses	railroad	broom	machine
bridges	track	sweeping	
goes	wheelchair		

16. _____

17. _____

18. _____

19. _____

20. _____

Worksheet 8-06

I. Describe each picture with a complete English sentence.

1.   2.   3.   4.   5.

1. _____

2. _____

3. _____

4. _____

5. _____

II. Yes or No?

_____ 6. A cow is a pet.

_____ 7. A bear does not belong to anyone.

_____ 8. All dogs are black.

_____ 9. A woman's pet belongs to the woman.

_____10. A boy's dog belongs to the boy.

_____11. Some girls' skirts are black.

_____12. Some women's dresses are blue.

_____13. All birds are pets.

_____14. Almost all umbrellas are green.

_____15. All animals are pets.

III. Write a complete English sentence using one or more words from the list.

belong	petting	girl's
belongs	farmer	girls'
pet	farmer's	

16. _____

17. _____

18. _____

19. _____

20. _____

Pets and Clothes; Possessive Adjectives and Pronouns   **ENGLISH**

I. Describe each picture with a complete English sentence.

1.	2.	3.	4.	5.

1. _____

2. _____

3. _____

4. _____

5. _____

II. Yes or No?

_____ 6. A woman is older than a girl.

_____ 7. A boy is older than a man.

_____ 8. A baby is older than an adult.

_____ 9. A tiger can run faster than a turtle.

_____10. A tiger has more spots than a leopard.

_____11. Sitting on a chair at home is dangerous.

_____12. Bald people have more hair than other people.

_____13. A dog can run faster than a cow.

_____14. Most men are taller than trees.

_____15. Motorcycles have fewer wheels than trucks.

III. Write a complete English sentence using one or more words from the list.

either	shortest	youngest	near	fastest	fewest	spots	striped	fight
leopard	highest	low	darkest	happiest	wettest	stripes	rather	home
taller	oldest	lowest	lightest	longest	coldest	spotted	dangerous	

16. _____

17. _____

18. _____

19. _____

20. _____

ENGLISH   **Comparative and Superlative Adjectives**

Worksheet 8-08

I. Describe each picture with a complete English sentence.

1. _____

2. _____

3. _____

4. _____

5. _____

II. Yes or No?

_____ 6. An airplane can fly far from the ground.

_____ 7. An airplane can fly on the ground.

_____ 8. People can stand close together.

_____ 9. A girl can have a pet.

_____10. It is dangerous to walk too close to a fire.

_____11. Most airplanes fly near the ground.

_____12. It is dangerous to get too close to a lion.

_____13. It is dangerous to get too close to a sofa.

_____14. A bird can fly near the ground.

_____15. A couple can sit close to each other.

III. Write a complete English sentence using one or more words from the list.

far   houses   closer
farther   close   apart

16. _____

17. _____

18. _____

19. _____

20. _____

Near and Far; Comparative Forms of Adjectives   **ENGLISH**

Worksheet 8-09

I. Describe each picture with a complete English sentence.

1. _____ **2.** _____ **3.** _____ **4.** _____ **5.** _____

1. _____

2. _____

3. _____

4. _____

5. _____

II. Yes or No?

bakery

mosque

bank

factory

hospital   church

_____ 6. The mosque is beside the hospital.

_____ 7. The bakery is around the corner from the bank.

_____ 8. The bank is beside the mosque.

_____ 9. The hospital is down the street from the church.

_____ 10. The bakery is beside the hospital.

_____ 11. The factory is around the corner from the church.

_____ 12. The bank is beside the bakery.

_____ 13. The bakery is a block down the street from the bank.

_____ 14. The church is across the street from the hospital.

_____ 15. The bakery is across the street from the mosque.

III. Write a complete English sentence using one or more words from the list.

restaurant	library	synagogue	hotel	movie	stop	Hindu	factory
airport	hospital	pharmacy	bakery	theater	subway	temple	university
playground	gas	supermarket	corner	block	mosque	prison	

16. _____

17. _____

18. _____

19. _____

20. _____

ENGLISH

Locations; Prepositions

Worksheet 8-10

I. Describe each picture with a complete English sentence.

1.   2.   3.   4.   5.

1. _____

2. _____

3. _____

4. _____

5. _____

II. Yes or No?

_____ 6. Streets can end.

_____ 7. Streets can fork.

_____ 8. Two blocks is more than three blocks.

_____ 9. A hospital is bigger than a house.

_____10. When a street forks, you do not go straight ahead.

_____11. Going around the corner is farther than going five blocks.

_____12. Going three blocks is farther than going one block.

_____13. Going across the street is farther than going four blocks.

_____14. A gas station is bigger than a hospital.

_____15. All subway stops are four blocks away from each other.

III. Write a complete English sentence using one or more words from the list.

do	your	school	until
blocks	ahead	forks	ends

16. _____

17. _____

18. _____

19. _____

20. _____

Worksheet 8-11

I. Describe each picture with a complete English sentence.

1.
2.
3.
4.
5.

1. _____

2. _____

3. _____

4. _____

5. _____

II. Yes or No?

_____ 6. Climbing a ladder is not dangerous at all.

_____ 7. Riding a bicycle is not dangerous at all.

_____ 8. Playing the guitar is very dangerous.

_____ 9. Putting on a shirt is dangerous.

_____10. Wearing a hat is dangerous.

_____11. Most people wear a shirt that is too small.

_____12. Some children can jump rope.

_____13. Some children play the guitar.

_____14. Babies can read books.

_____15. Nobody can climb a ladder.

III. Write a complete English sentence using one or more words from the list.

| reading | jumping | digging | wearing | holding | putting |
| fishing | drinking | climbing | playing | picking | running |

16. _____

17. _____

18. _____

19. _____

20. _____

Word Search 8: 1-5

ALLEY
BRIDGES
BROOM
CALLED
COLORED
CONTINENT
COUNTRY
FIRST
FOURTH
GOES
HIGHWAY
HOLE
LAST
LIKE
LOWER
MACHINE
MAP
PLANET
RAILROAD
SECOND
SHAPES
SWEEPING
THIRD
TOWARD
UPPER

```
A F S E C O N D U P P E R
E I H C O U N T R Y Z U Q
H R A I L R O A D F P O J
D S P I O I L B D A M A P
X T E E R B M R W F Z L C
R D S W E E P I N G I L S
G O E S D T N D I N M E V
M A T M T H I G H W A Y F
Z C O N T I N E N T C N O
L O W E R R A S F N H R U
I L A S T D H O L E I X R
K B R O O M S P L A N E T
E M D N S R C A L L E D H
```

Word Search 8: 6-11

AHEAD
AIRPORT
BELONGS
CORNER
DANGEROUS
EITHER
FACTORY
FAR
FARMER
FIGHT
GAS
HIGHEST
HOME
HOSPITAL
LOW
PHARMACY
PLAYGROUND
PRISON
RATHER
RESTAURANT
SCHOOL
SUBWAY
SUPERMARKET
UNTIL
YOUR

```
R H S Y U P H A R M A C Y
Q O C I F A R M E R D V W
G M S V A H E A D F P P L
Q E T V H O S P I T A L T
A I R P O R T S U B W A Y
S U P E R M A R K E T Y O
C O R N E R U S B H B G U
H E I T H E R A T H E R R
O F S H E F A R V Z L O F
O L O W D A N G E R O U S
L U N T I L T A Q H N N H
F A C T O R Y S Z E G D V
F I G H T H I G H E S T G
```

Crossword 8: 1-5

Across

1. It looks ___ a triangle.
5. not sunset
7. Most of the flower is red, but ___ of it is white.
10. a musical instrument
11. Beside the street is the _____.
12. The road ___ toward the house.
14. not that
17. She is neither talking ___ eating.
20. She was wearing a sweater, but she is not wearing it ___.
22. Saturn is a _____.
24. She is _____ talking nor eating.

Down

1. not first
2. ___ of the singers are girls, but some are women.
3. She is _____ the sidewalk with a broom.
4. This planet is _____ Saturn.
6. Cars drive on a ____.
8. not above
9. The _____ number in 503 is a five.
13. second, third, _____
15. digging a ____
16. father and ___
18. ___ one of us is singing.
19. first, second, ____
21. __, two, three
23 It looks like a square, but it is ___.

Crossword 8: 6-11

Across

2. This cat _____ to a little girl.
8. an animal
9. The dog is white with black ____.
10. The church is ___ the street from the bank.
14. It is _____ to jump off a horse.
15. Go down the street _____ it forks.
16. This dog is her ___.
19. ___ makes smoke.
21. The hotel is around the _____.
22. not closer
23. not longest

Down

1. Go straight _____.
3. Go down the street until it ____.
4. Turn left at the ____ station.
5. fast, faster, ____
6. do not go
7. cold, colder, ____
11. not shorter
12. not the most but the ____
13. The airplane is flying ___, near the ground.
17. ____ animal has stripes?
18. not far
19. When the street _____, turn right.
20. not together
21. Someone is driving the ___